Scraps from the Father's Banquet Table

Spiritual Food for Thought

by
Susan Ceraldi Jaquith

To Jenny –
Enjoy the read!
Sue Jaquith

Inscript

Published by Inscript Books
a division of Dove Christian Publishers
P.O. Box 611
Bladensburg, MD 20710-0611
www.inscriptpublishing.com

Inscript and the portrayal of a pen with script are trademarks of Dove Christian Publishers.

Book Design by Mark Yearnings

ISBN: 978-1-957497-04-4

Printed in the United States of America

I dedicate this book to my parents: Edmund and Mary (Mae) Ceraldi, who first taught me how to pray; and the joy of a really good meal gathered around the family banquet table.

And to my sister, Judy Wartschow, my first and life-long prayer partner.

"Taste and see that the Lord is good; blessed is the one who takes refuge in Him." (Psalm 34:8)

Contents

PART IV.

SOME "GOOD GOD" QUESTIONS

Introduction

The Holy Spirit has been prompting me to create this book for the past 40 years, bit by bit, inspiration by inspiration. I saved my notes along the way. Although I envisioned this book several decades ago, I could not get myself to actually write it for a variety of reasons. Struggles with procrastination aside, I had the overwhelming sense that there are already so many books out there that I would not have anything unique to add. Yet, the gentle prodding of the Holy Spirit (and my family) continued, so I continued.

It's funny, but I knew the title of this book long before it came together in my mind. It came from pondering the Gospel account (Matthew 15:27, Mark 7:28) that seems to make Jesus sound very cruel. There is a Samaritan woman who asks Jesus to heal her daughter, but she is not an Israelite. Jesus responds that He came for the children of Israel, not the "dogs." Really? Jesus' response here seems unusual, leaving me to wonder if there is a greater point to this encounter. The seemingly unoffended woman replies, "but even dogs are allowed to eat the scraps that fall beneath their masters' table." (*New Living Translation*, Matthew 15:27). Jesus commends her great faith and grants the healing she requested. I got to thinking that what is really amazing here is that even the scraps from God's table are more than enough to satisfy the hunger in any human being. And we are told that the Father's banquet table awaits us as part of heaven's joy. For an epicure like me who loves to eat and drink well, I could relate to this promise of delight.

I do believe there is an ultimate absolute Truth that underlies the chaos we find ourselves living in; a truth that is unchanging, and true whether we believe it or not. It calms me to hear Jesus say, "I am the Way, the Truth and the Life" (John 14:6). Finding this Truth is not always so obvious or absolute, and it may appear differently when seen through the different lives and perspectives of unique individuals. We all hear the same Word, yet understand and relate to it uniquely. God is infinite and we are finite. We try to hold on to the piece of revelation we have been given, and when shared, hopefully results in a broader glimpse of who God is. If each of us wrote a book, we still couldn't capture the full revelation of our beloved Father, His beloved Son, and the Holy Spirit that calls and leads us home to the loving Father's banquet table.

Since giving my life to Jesus and embarking on this spiritual journey, I have received inspired teachings and revelations from the Lord during my lifetime. I know they came from God because I know myself, that I am simply not capable of such thoughts or understanding. As insights came to me, I received them almost as if I was listening to a speaker, and I would jot down some notes from those moments. I was invited to give teachings at prayer groups or retreats, and I discovered that what I had already been receiving from the Lord in prayer was the topic on which I was being invited to teach! In this way, I began to learn that it was the Holy Spirit teaching me first, so I could then share what I had learned and teach others. Over the years I collected some of these teachings in a notebook and put them aside.

After retiring from my 35-year engineering career, I took my spiritual notebook off the shelf and realized that to keep it on my shelf, collecting dust, was a waste of a gift that had been given. It was like storing manna that God had provided to feed His people. It would be worth more in the hands of others who were also seeking guidance from the Holy Spirit; it could be anointed and come alive again and feed the hunger deep within other souls.

I pray you will be fed, blessed, loved, and even healed by these Scraps from the Father's Banquet Table, as I was when I first tasted His goodness and learned that He alone can satisfy my every need.

PART I.

CHOICES WE MAKE

My First Choice

Jesus Christ was and is the Father's great rescue mission. When we remember that Jesus and the Father are one, we begin to realize that when God sent His only Son Jesus, He sent Himself. And we are told that He did this because of His love for us.

Jesus revealed to the world the good news that God is our Father and that He loves us, and He wants to forgive our sins. God through Jesus entered our world to seek and save the lost. We are told in John 3:16 that God did not send Jesus to condemn the world, but rather to save the world. Perhaps John 3:16 has become so familiar to us that we no longer hear the power of its message.

Besides being born in human flesh so that He could die for us, Jesus also came to show us the Way, the Truth and the Life. Jesus is the Way back home to the Father. He is the Truth, which replaces all the lies and deception the evil one tries to lure us away with. He is the Life, eternal life, that when His body entered death He thereby extinguished death's grip on all of humanity, making death now a gateway back home to God and heaven rather than a permanent end of our life. Jesus not only enters our world, but He leaves it, through death. This is important and necessary to accomplish the plan of salvation. Equally important and necessary is His resurrection. If He didn't rise from the dead, then Jesus would have ended as other great men and women do, and He would not have succeeded in releasing humanity from death's permanent grip. This is amazing when we think about it: by entering death, He transformed it. Therefore, His victory paves for us the way back home.

We need to look at what it cost Jesus to die for me and for you. This happened vividly for me on Palm Sunday 1977, when the Holy Spirit opened my heart to really enter into the Passion gospel. This was the conversion that forever changed my life. In the Roman Catholic Church, the passion is read like a play, and the part of the crowd is assigned to the congregation. When we got to the part where the crowd shouted "Crucify Him," I couldn't say the words and I began to weep. I was overcome with sorrow that we would cry out for His crucifixion, and everything in me wanted to shout "NOOOOO." And I really was there in spirit; I could feel the pressure of the crowd pressing in around me, I could smell the sweat. I was immersed in the mentality of the crowd and how frightening that felt. Then at the cross, I really saw Him; I saw His hands, hands that healed so many, nailed firmly to the cross, as if we were saying "stop healing us!" I saw His feet, feet that walked all over to bring the good news, nailed to cross, as if we were saying "stop finding us." I saw His head crowned with thorns – the great dishonor of that, mocking Him as king, rather than bending our knee in love and respect. But the absolute ultimate atrocity for me, the thing that made me crazy, was seeing people spit on Him. I remembered how, in the Old Testament, Moses could not even directly look at the face of God and live. But here on the cross, the face of God is covered in human spit.

You know, when you realize that Jesus was still God, that He was still all-powerful, that at any moment He could have cried out "ENOUGH!" and that He could have destroyed all those who were beating, mocking and killing Him, you realize how much humility and love was in His heart to choose to surrender His power so He could save us, rather than vindicate and free Himself. I cannot comprehend such humility. Surrendered power is the most powerful power of all. Jesus did not surrender His power to Pilate, or to the Jews, or to the crowd. He surrendered His power to His Father's will.

If it takes such humility from God to give us the gift of salvation at the cross, then it should come as no surprise that it takes humility on our part to come to the cross to receive that gift. And Jesus prays, "Father forgive them, they know not what they do." He is saying, "Father, please don't stop loving them...they really don't know what they are doing."

We likely can never fully realize what we are saved from exactly, but we cannot deny that we see a vicious and repetitive cycle of sin and woundedness around us. We are both wounded and we wound (hurt) others. Jesus interrupts that cycle with one word - FORGIVE-NESS. We look to the cross and hear Him say, as it were, THE BUCK STOPS HERE.

After Jesus said "Father, into your hands I commend my Spirit," He breathed His last. I feel that moment every time...the last breath of Jesus on earth as the Son of Man. But that breath was meant to be received by all who would come to believe in Him.

It cost Jesus a great deal to give us the Holy Spirit, so that we will have a constant guide within us, Jesus Himself, reminding us of all He taught us. In my own life, I deal with depression – I tend to focus on what still needs doing and I struggle to feel satisfied, and grateful even, for what is. I have to say to myself, "Jesus died for my joy; why am I choosing depression?" Or, "Jesus died for my freedom from x, y, z...so why am I still choosing to be enslaved by x, y, z?"

So I made the fundamental choice for Jesus. I chose to love Him in return.

That began my journey of making many choices for Jesus.

PRAYER

No matter what choices you have made in the past, somehow you have been led by God to this moment, now.

No matter where you are at this time in your life, you can choose God.

Choose God.

You are free to choose to believe in God's gift of salvation for you.

Believe!

You are free to choose Jesus as your Savior, and to accept His gift of eternal life.

Accept Jesus as your Savior and receive His gift of eternal life.

You are free to choose Jesus as your Lord, to follow God's will over your own.

Choose Jesus as your Lord!

You are free to choose to believe He is alive!

Believe He is alive!

You are free to choose to love Him in return.

Love Jesus.

Amen.

The 2 Gardens – Eden and Gethsemane

Think of home as the Garden of Eden, before the fall. The Garden of Eden was a place of creation, great beauty, bountiful and plentiful fruit, and best of all, it was the sacred place where we were created to dwell with God. In Genesis 3:8, we see that God took daily walks with Adam in the Garden. Can you imagine that? How intimate! What friendship! It was all about God's relationship with His beloved Adam and Eve. There was only one command given…only ONE!!!! They were told by God that they could eat from any tree in the garden except for the Tree of the Knowledge of Good and Evil. God did not want them to taste and experience the disastrous results of eating from that tree. He did not want to poison His beloved. He did not want them ever to be sick, to feel pain, to experience the anguish of guilt and shame, or to die.

I find it very interesting how the serpent came to Eve, while she was gazing at and very close to the tree. That is the first step towards falling into sin…getting close to it. It seems the first temptation was getting anywhere near the tree that God said not to touch. And that is where the serpent was coiled. I believe she entered into his territory. That is why Catholics pray to "avoid the near occasions of sin" when reciting the Act of Contrition prayer, as that is where our act of sin begins.

So what was the temptation in the garden anyway? I believe that the real temptation was for Adam and Eve to not believe God's word to them. In Genesis 2:17 God said, "you must not eat of this tree or you will surely die." That wasn't a trick or a threat; rather it was a statement of truth. Just like if God were to say, "Don't jump off the top of the 10 story building or you will fall down and hit the ground and die." If I jump and die, did God kill me?

The temptation was to doubt God's motive, to distrust Him and His nature – to wonder as the serpent proposes that God is not really good, and His motive is not for love of them but rather to RULE OVER THEM! The serpent says, "If you eat of this tree you will BE LIKE GOD! And God doesn't want you to be like Him but rather to be subject to Him." And sadly, the great irony is that it is actually Satan's motive – to control and rule over us, and to destroy us.

We know how this goes…Eve succumbs to the temptation, and once she has eaten of the apple, she has this need to get Adam to eat of it as well. Perhaps a delayed reaction – it appeared to her that nothing bad happened and she couldn't wait to share with Adam the "new truth" the serpent just revealed to her. She was going to set them both free from…free from *what* exactly? God's love? His presence? His generosity? His protection? His provision? Their relationship with Him? From eternal life without toil, sickness, pain or death? It boggles my mind sometimes, but it shouldn't, because we do the same thing when we think we will find freedom apart from God and His Word.

We see the immediate effects of this wrong choice when they no longer want to walk with God. For the first time since they were created, they hide from God. When they no longer show up for their daily walk, God cries out "Adam, where are you?" Now God is all knowing, so of course He knew where Adam was. But what God also knew was that Adam was lost…for the first time…lost in the garden…hiding in shame and guilt. God knew exactly what had been unleashed on His beautiful creation, and how it had to have happened. Today, in our time in history, God similarly calls to each one of us, wherever we are lost and hiding in guilt and shame, asking, "Where are you in relation to Me?"

Many years later, we find Jesus in another garden - the Garden of Gethsemane. Jesus is fully aware of His impending arrest, aware that Judas had already betrayed Him, and He was fully aware of what was to come – that He would die as the Paschal Lamb on Passover to atone for the sins of the humanity He loves. I am not sure if He anticipated the depth of loneliness and pain that would come with His sacrifice, but it began when His few intimate friends could not stay awake with Him for even one hour after He asked them to be with Him. Little did they know that this was the last hour they would have with Him before His death. They slept, He prayed.

Scripture tells us that He was sweating drops of blood (Luke 22:44) due to the anguish of knowing that the time was now. It is interesting to note that there is a condition believed to be hematohidrosis, diagnosed in a number of people facing and prior to their execution, caused frequently by extreme stress. And He cried out to His Father that if it were possible, please let this cup pass from Him. He cried out in the same way that we cry out. I remember the sorrow I felt the first time I realized that Jesus first shed His blood for us here in this garden.

As He cried out He prayed "yet not my will, but yours be done" (Luke 22:42). Jesus maintained His complete faith and trust in His Father, choosing to believe in God's will over His own desires. In so choosing, He attests that God's motives are based in love, and that God's motive is always for good. Jesus affirms that *this* is the Truth, the Truth that sets us free when we believe it, the Truth that will bring liberation to all who believe. Jesus, like us, was tempted to do things another way, an easier way, a way different from God's way. However, Jesus chose the Father's will, not His own, and in so doing, He reversed the choice made by Adam and Eve in the other garden, the Garden of Eden. We don't often realize the suffering of Jesus in the garden.

When reflecting on the Gardens of Eden and Gethsemane, we are reflecting on opposites: Eden vs. Gethsemane; evil vs. good; lies vs. truth; pride vs. humility; death vs. life. We have the power, NOW, at this very moment to choose good over evil, to choose God's spoken Truth over lies and deception and the lure of the glamor of evil; to choose life by obeying God's Word, to choose to believe that the Father's motive and purpose for our lives is for good, not evil; to choose to accept the gift of salvation at the cross. We have the choice to pray in the spirit of Jesus in the Garden of Gethsemane, trusting in the Father's will over our own, rather than to play underneath the forbidden tree in the Garden of Eden. It is hard to grasp the consequences of that choice in our personal lives as well as its impact on the whole world, but as we make such choices little by little, we come to better appreciate the amazing and wonderful difference they make.

PRAYER

We can all relate to feeling lost at times. Imagine yourself in the Garden of Eden, and you are hiding, or lost. Hear God call your name. "Sue, where are you? Bob, where are you? [Your name], where are you?" Hear the longing in God's call to both let you know He is searching for you, and that He shows up every day to take that walk with you. He longs to be in relationship with you, and your relationship with Him is restored because of Jesus.

Choose to show up for the walk in the garden with the God who loves you, and let Him show you the wonders in His plan for your life, and the future full of hope that He has chosen for you.

Thank you Jesus for making it possible for me to return to my heavenly home after my death, but also even right now, through prayer, to walk with You while I am still exiled here on planet Earth.

Amen.

3

Dealing with Fear

We learn in Proverbs 9:10 that "The fear of the Lord is the beginning of wisdom." That sense of the word "fear" is one of awe and reverence. That is not the context of this reflection. I am talking about the kind of fear that Jesus spoke about, when He walked among us. One of the most frequent commands from His heart to ours in the gospels is "Fear not", or the like, "Do not be afraid, it is I." "Fear not, I am with you." "Why were you afraid?" For all our sins and failings and human condition, that is what He saw when He looked at us. Perhaps Jesus is exposing fear to be the root of all our fatal flaws; a gnawing fear of our own inadequacy, and an inability to believe in a God whose motive is purely good and who loves us as we are. Jesus did not say over and over again, "Lay down your pride." What He said instead was, "Give me your fear."

The "12-step program", used to manage living with addictions (most notably Alcoholics Anonymous (AA)), has an acronym for the word **FEAR** - **F**alse **E**vidence **A**ppearing **R**eal. These four simple words give us a profound teaching about fear. Isn't that an awesome way to think of Fear? It addresses the question of why are we afraid, providing the answer that we are afraid because we are believing some lie, something that is false, something that is not true. It also offers us the possibility that if we can identify the underlying lie, we can realign our thinking with the truth.

Often present challenges evoke FEAR in us, based on painful memories from our past, especially from our childhood. The child within us has tucked away in its memory something that hurt us, and that hurt was very real. The painful memory is a true experience, and we don't want to dig it up again. There is a real fear of vulnerability, of being hurt again. Some of us have vowed never to be hurt again in this same way. But the way we coped as a child is likely no longer working for us as adults, and we feel an anxiety because there always seem to be obstacles in our path to developing into our adult purpose and calling. We have a vague sense of our purpose but often feel paralyzed, stuck, or just plain afraid to step into it. There is a feeling of being trapped, blocked, or hidden, or a sense that no one can hear me, or worse, that I have no voice at all.

We don't want to see for ourselves and especially we don't want others to see it, as if how bad something was is somehow a statement of how bad I really am. Some of the underlying fears that plague us are that: I really am *not good*, I am *unlovable*, I am just *a mess and always will be*, there is *something inherently wrong with me*, I am a *bad child*, I am the *one mistake God ever made!* We experience a fear of abandonment, of guilt and of shame.

Another fear that many of us suffer from is the fear that I am *not worthy or valid*, I am *not important*. Because we learned to focus so much on others, and not on ourselves, it feels wrong to take care of me. To pay attention to "My Self" is a new thing, and new things seem wrong at first. *"I'm not a real person entitled to be loved."* That is a lie that must be overcome to displace this fear.

Perhaps you suffer from the pervasive doubt that the concept of healing is even real. You have learned to have a *Fear of Disappointment*. "I don't even want to try this. It won't work for me." This fear is often accompanied by feelings of hopelessness. We can believe the lie that there is something very wrong and different about me, and we think things like "you don't know me and how bad I really am." If I dare to believe that healing is possible, and then I seemingly am not healed, then I will be worse off than before. That will make me depressed. I will think I have failed. I will believe that *I am a failure*, or that it is too difficult for me to even try to overcome my fears. This is the *Fear of Failure*.

Or then there is an opposite fear: maybe healing *will* work! So this fear can become "who will I be after I'm healed?" "Will I be committing myself to more responsibility than I can handle or want?" This is a *Fear of Loss of Self*, and it can overpower us because our definition of self is often fragile and fragmented, to the extent that we are afraid to probe or change our way of thinking and coping.

1 John 4:18 states that "Perfect love casts out fear." When we enter into the love relationship with Jesus and His Father, our fear diminishes as God's love fills our hearts. And it is not a love that is given to us because we are worthy or perfect - quite the opposite. I remember the tears and sobs that came out of me when I heard Fr. Brennan Manning preach, "Do you believe God loves you just the way you are, and not the way you should be...or think you should be? Do you believe He expects more failure from you than you do from yourself?" I just couldn't believe that such unconditional love could be given. Especially because I know I don't love that way. But this is the perfect love that casts out fear. We need to let it in.

The Father sent Jesus to us while we were still lost and exiled here on planet Earth. We love Him because He first loved us (1 John 4:19). After Jesus' ascension to heaven, the Father gave the Holy Spirit to the believers gathered together in the upper room on Pentecost. This is the way Jesus remains with us always while we live out our exile here on planet Earth. The Holy Spirit also leads us into community, and

Jesus told us that "wherever two or more of you are gathered, there I am in your midst." (Matthew 18:20). For whatever reason, God's reason, community is meant to be part of our spiritual journey, and the presence of Jesus is always with us.

Consider this example of community. Imagine yourself walking alone in a dark, dense forest, and that you are lost. Feel the dread of your aloneness and the sense of being lost. Every little sound or motion evokes new fear and you don't know which way to turn. Now imagine that one other person is with you, a dear friend or loved one. Can you feel how the fear diminishes when there is another beating heart beside you, a hand to hold or a person to talk to? Now imagine that you are in a group together on this walk. Instead of a fear-filled experience, now it becomes an interesting journey, maybe even a little fun and exciting, an experience to be shared! There may even be a belly laugh or two before the daylight comes and your path is found. It becomes apparent that fear is diminished when there is love and you are in a loving community. This is how we are meant to live while here on planet earth awaiting Jesus's return.

When I was a child, I always loved the story about the Prince and the Pauper. I never realized until I found Jesus that this was a story about what Jesus did for me, and for you. He was the Son of God, and He came from heaven, a palace and kingdom the likes of which we have never seen on earth, to enter into our exile here on planet earth, where we are like paupers wearing the rags of our sin, our poverty and our sense of aimlessness. Jesus is the Prince, who exchanges His royal status and garments for us to wear, and He wears our rags instead. He takes on our sin so that we can find our way back to the Kingdom of God. He clothes us in His righteousness rather than our rags. We can only exchange our rags for His garments if we can see and admit that we are truly wearing rags.

It is scary to be the pauper without ever meeting the Prince. But once we meet the Prince and realize that He is willing to exchange His life for ours, simply because He loves us and wants to be with us and to share His glory and riches with us, it is then that our fear can begin to be transformed to gratitude and acceptance of perfect love, which casts out fear.

Choose the exchange!

PRAYER

Take a moment to be with the Lord in prayer. Ask the Holy Spirit to enter into this prayer time and to begin to reveal to you an area where you sense you are not free from fear. Consider possible fears that can be dominating your behavior and/or belief system.

What are you afraid of now, at this moment in your life?

- Fear of failure?

- Fear of disappointment?

- Fear of being unworthy?

- Fear of being inferior, or incompetent?

- Fear of abandonment?

What might be the lie that you are believing? For example:

Do you think that God cannot or will not love you because of your inadequacies, or your tendency towards sin?

Do you believe that there is something inherently wrong with you?

Do you believe that you are somehow the one person that God cannot love?

To counter the lies behind such fears, consider the truth that is based on God's love and His Word to us and replace the lie with the truth:

- 1 John 4:18 - Perfect love casts out fear.

- Isaiah 43 - God made me, is my true parent, and loves me as I am and not as I should be. He is with me.

- God expects more failure from me than I do from myself.

- A perfect person is not loveable, or real. Don't try to be perfect. Accept your limitations, celebrating that "God is God, and I am not!"

Replace the lie with the truth.

No one knows you better than the Father knows you, and No one loves you more than He does.

Amen.

The Paralysis of Regret

Regret is a painful word. It indicates losses, mistakes made, or dreams abandoned. Regret can come from being broken by our own sinful choices as well as from wounds caused by the sins of others. It is a word that seems to say that you can't go back and do it all over again. But the victory of Jesus tells us that our God is greater even than our mistakes.

Mistakes can only be part of the past. While I stand in the present moment, there is always the hope that the next choice I make will align with God's perfect way, and that my choice will lead me toward the fulfillment of my purpose here on earth, and deeper into my relationship with Jesus, rather than take me on a detour that will inevitably lead to consequences that I do not want in my life. When I think of my mistakes, I am remembering the past. There is certainly an appropriate need for this, for we can only repent for what was done in the past. But once we truly come to terms with a mistake, and by coming to terms I mean simply admitting it was wrong, then I need to enter into the gift that Jesus died to give me – the forgiveness of my sin. That is part of the Good News – that Jesus' death, burial and resurrection, resulting in victory over sin and death, works even for my mistakes. Do you believe that God is greater than your mistakes?

It is hard to feel "good" when we have to live with the consequences of our bad choices. Jesus even goes so far as to accompany us in our consequences. He helps us to carry our acquired life circumstances and always seeks to work for good in our lives. One of my favorite Scripture verses is from Romans 8:28 "All things work together for good to those who love God."

So here we find ourselves again, back to whether or not we love God. That is always the fundamental choice in our lives. All decisions somehow can be traced back to this one.

There is also the kind of regret we experience because of the wrongs done to us. It is extremely difficult to live with painful consequences that come from having been hurt by others, especially if someone has affected the course of my life, or destroyed my personhood. I believe that only Jesus can heal these wounds because He models the way out from His own passion on the Cross. He shows us that we have a choice to forgive those who have hurt us, thereby offering us a way out of a lifetime of reliving and suffering from the same wound for the rest of our lives. We are invited to forgive others for the wrongs they have done to us rather than allow them to keep hurting us over and over again by not letting go of our right to be angry and allowing God to heal us.

The way to be healed of regret is to choose repentance and forgiveness. When we repent of our own wrongdoing we can then accept Jesus' sacrifice for us and allow ourselves to be forgiven. When we forgive someone for wrongs that were done to us (even if the person who harmed us was our own self!) we can then let go of reliving it so it doesn't keep happening to us over and over again. To be stuck in the past, however, and continue to nurse regret without the intention of seeking to repent and accept forgiveness, will paralyze us in our journey.

We cannot go back and undo the past. Peter can never go back and refuse to deny Jesus three times in the wee hours of Good Friday morning...the cock already crowed. Judas can never go back and refuse to betray His Lord. He already received his thirty pieces of blood money, which sent him beyond regret and into complete despair and subsequent suicide. We can only choose to put into action the gift that Jesus gave us from the Cross...the invitation to acknowledge and repent of our wrongdoing and accept God's forgiveness of those wrongs.

We have all failed along the way and hindsight is always so clear. We may get angry with ourselves and want to give up. There is the lie that says, "you have already failed, why bother anymore, your dreams and potential are gone now." That is when we need to bring the broken pieces of our hopes and dreams to Jesus, and ask Him to show us the way to move forward, out of the paralysis of regret. In the gospels (Matthew 9:5, Luke 5:23), Jesus healed the paralytic saying, which is easier to say to a person...your sins are forgiven? Or Rise up and Walk." Hear the Lord say to you now, "Your sins are forgiven! Rise up and walk."

PRAYER

It serves us well to remember the sting of regret to the extent that we consider our future choices in light of where past choices have taken us.

What comes to your remembrance when you think of past regrets?

Where do you feel the sting of regret in your life?

Decisions are often made hastily in the moment. There is great pressure on us to decide, and great temptation to only consider immediate gratification. If we can use the sting of past regrets to help us pause and make more prayerful decisions, then we are beginning to grow in wisdom.

What painful circumstances are you in because of past choices you have made?

Is there a choice in front of you at this time in your life?

Consider your choices

Ask "Will my decision lead me closer to God's ways, or away?"

Holy Spirit, I willingly come into Your presence. Help me to feel your presence and peace and love. I ask you to bring to my mind that which Jesus wants to heal me of at this moment. I repent and ask for forgiveness for [your specific sin]. I offer forgiveness to [anyone that I blame or feel has caused me harm resulting in consequences in my life that are hurtful to me now].

I ask for the grace to move on and live the rest of my life free of this [guilt, anger, hatred, etc.] I choose to believe and discover anew Your miraculous power that not only restores me, but is working now to even bring good out of the circumstances, wounds and mistakes that I so deeply regret.

Amen.

5

"Caring" About Apathy

As apathy is the absence of caring, I thought it a clever title, and it is a state of interest to me, because I am typically passionate about anything I care about! I suppose I should be grateful that I "cared enough" to explore this topic, as it is worth exploring.

Apathy can set in after we experience multiple disappointments or failures, which often result in a lack of belief or interest in the "cause." In Revelations 3:16 in the letter to the church of Laodicea, Jesus says that He would rather we were either hot or cold, but lukewarm He will spit out of His mouth. Jesus wants us to care, about issues, about people, about ourselves, and about God.

Being apathetic can derail the true purpose of our lives. I can tell when passion wanes because I start to feel without purpose or meaning. The first step out of apathy is to recognize it as the culprit it is, the Devourer of our dreams and God-given potential.

When I first chose to fully enter into relationship with God, I was young – 20 years old – and filled with enthusiasm that had me bouncing off the proverbial walls. I was sure that in no time I would be able to say the perfect prayer that would result in paraplegics standing up out of their wheelchairs because I knew beyond all doubt that I had connected with the Living God. I took risks, went out on a limb, and was a "fool for Christ!" After many failures, or let's be kind and call them "lessons learned," I learned that I could not possess or control God. The journey is supposed to be God saying to me "Here I am… follow Me", but I had it reversed, so that it was me saying to God "Here I am… follow me." What a difference the capital M can make!

Apathy on our spirit is a lot like dust on furniture – it settles on us, and covers the natural gleam of who we really are. And we get used to it. It isn't until someone jokingly takes their finger and writes the words "Dust Me" do we realize how dull we have become. The good news is that it doesn't take a lot of effort to remove the dust, but it requires that we notice it, that we do not like it there, and that we choose to get up and get rid of it.

You may have been very disappointed after stepping out in faith, only to feel powerless or ineffective, or humiliated. You may have once had a vibrant faith, believing that you could do greater things than Jesus, because He said we would do so, but then found that you could not. Perhaps we are evaluating our effectiveness by worldly standards and not by God's. Either way, no matter what happens, the results are up to Him. We are called to say yes, to step up to the plate when called, to get up off the ground after falling, to try again and again and again…seventy times seven times if necessary…and dust ourselves off to be equipped by the Holy Spirit once again. No matter your past, you should never settle for a lackluster faith journey…dare to become the person God created you to be.

Many years ago I was dealing with depression and I pretty much had given up on ever thinking I could find my place in this world, let alone bear fruit for God's kingdom. As I was struggling to find a healthy relationship that I so much wanted to find, I had one of those life-changing moments where Jesus's words in the gospels leapt out as being just for me. In Gospel of Mark 5:41, Jesus goes into the room of a little girl that everyone believes is dead. He is mocked when He asks if He can go to her. When He enters, He takes her hand and gently speaks "Little Girl, arise!" I felt Him take my hand, and gently help me to get up and care again about life – my life – and to allow Him to give me a second chance, a new beginning. "Behold I make all things new." I think Jesus's words in this gospel account can also speak to the apathetic spirit that grips us for many different reasons.

PRAYER

Take a moment to recall a time that you did something out of blind obedience, that though others thought this was the right thing for you to do, and you did it, but the action just wasn't flowing from that place of caring and passion within you.

Now, take a moment to recall a moment or period in your life where you were very in touch with your own enthusiasm, and had the sense of the Lord empowering you to do something that you had a passion to do, regardless of whether others thought what you were doing was right at the time. Get in touch with your feelings about the tasks and the feelings you had about it.

Now look at your present moment…where are you in relation to the two scenarios above? Are you still acting out of a place of resignation…or obedience to someone else's idea of what you should be doing? Or are you feeling the movement of the Holy Spirit, working with the desires in your own heart and yearnings to contribute in a certain way?

Come Lord Jesus! In the Name of Jesus, I renounce the spirit of apathy and all its tentacles that are stifling the joy and purpose of my life. I renounce the memories of failure and disappointment and I again choose to care and to seek and find the calling of your Spirit within me.

Apathy creeps in when we are no longer in touch with our passion and our first love. We have to take out the dust cloth and remove the layers of dust that have caked onto our true vibrant selves to be able to feel again.

Amen.

6

Wrestling with Anger and Resentment

Most people in my life would never suspect that two of the demons I wrestle with quite frequently are anger and resentment. I know they are two different "animals" but for me they are married and function together as a very oppressive "one-two" punch. On the outside I probably appear more depressed than angry or resentful, but you know how it is – only you, and Jesus, know exactly what is at the root of "You."

When I experience it, my depression is really rooted in and driven by an anger that I cannot resolve – so strong sometimes that it can take away my ability to love; and a resentment that makes me feel despair – so strong sometimes that it can take away my hope for my future. It is only because of my knowledge that Jesus died to overcome both of these for my sake that I choose to move forward, because I don't ever want to waste the saving power and freedom that is available to me through His death and resurrection to make positive changes in my own personal life. It is because of Him that I know that I can bring these demons to the foot of His cross, and that they will have to die there. Before they die there, however, they do wreak a lot of havoc!

What does this mean in practical terms? How do you bring a demon within yourself to the foot of the cross for it to die? The challenge and the everlasting call is again in the invitation for ME to come to the cross. I can't bring my demons there unless and until I can bring myself there. And die to my false self I must. The demons do not die until I align myself with Jesus, and stand firm on my choice to be free.

So, when I feel wronged, and anger begins to bubble within, my tendency is to toy with that for a while. I give into it. I feel it. It is not comfortable or pleasant, but it is oh so righteous; meaning I seem to need to validate that I truly have been wronged, or misunderstood, or overlooked. What I have started to realize is that the anger makes me miserable, and then I feel guilty that my love is blocked in some way. Just like when our physical body is blocked, and we are hanging onto waste that really was meant to be gotten rid of, we need to see our anger in that same way. I do not mean that we don't have valid issues to resolve, but nurturing the anger is never the way to resolution. We want it to pass through us as soon as possible.

I started to notice that the anger that I am feeling is often really directed at myself, not at another person or situation. Why might that be? Perhaps it is because I am often unable to confront the person who has hurt me, or to ask for what I need or want, so in frustration I get angry instead! I envy people that can pick up the phone and ask for whatever they want, be it information or help, or confront a wrong done to them as soon as it happens.

I was in a situation recently (I can't share it in order to protect the "innocent") but let me say that I felt terribly overlooked and left out when I felt I had given so much, and considered other's feelings above my own so many times that I was surprised to have been so left out. It wasn't until I was able to ask on my own behalf for what I wished others had thought of on my behalf that I felt a complete lifting of the heaviness of the anger. So speaking up for my own need helped to free me from being angry, and the inevitable resentment of the people and situation that brought me pain. For me, resentment follows the anger. Anger is a big burst of passion that overtakes me, then I try to deny and dismiss it; whereas resentment is like a seeping slow poison that keeps me sick for a very long time…like even for years.

I wish I could tell you that when I asked for what I needed that I got it, but I did not! What I did get (besides the amazing liberation from my anger) was a better understanding of the situation and why I might not have been on the radar screen the way I thought I deserved to be. That understanding allowed love and forgiveness to begin to trickle in. I can't lie to you, it is a constant choice to not pick it up again, and nurse it back into destructive power. But why oh why would I want to do that…to myself? See, that's the rub! My anger and resentment only hurts me, not the other person. It keeps me stuck and constantly hurt by re-experiencing the painful assault over and over again, instead of just that once.

Jesus is no trickster. He does not suggest forgiveness as an un-achievable goal to aspire to. He did not choose forgiveness on the cross because it was easy for Him to do so. He chose it because He knew it was the victory path, and the only way to get free of the feelings of anger, rage, powerlessness, depression, and despair that He must have been tempted to feel as He bore all of our sorrows. He chose forgiveness as the way out and back to His Father. "Father forgive them, they know not what they do" is one of the greatest teachings we have from Jesus about how to live in this world and rise above the evil that will always try to devour us and detour us from the Way, the Truth and the Life.

PRAYER

Ask the Holy Spirit to reveal to you a specific situation or time when you became very angry. Not just irritated, but when you felt anger "take over".

Is there a repetitive pattern to your anger? Are there unique triggers that cause you to become angry? Think of patterns of your reactions when hurt, or when feeling powerless or depressed. If there is a pattern, can you recall when it first began in your life?

Bring to the Lord any memory or memories that surface. Don't go digging for it, but if there is something that you become aware of, ask Jesus to enter into that situation to show you more about what happened to you or in you. Ask Him to heal this event in your life. This will likely be an ongoing process, but if the Lord is showing it to you, you can be sure He intends to move in your life to bring you freedom and peace in this area. Perhaps you need to forgive someone, or yourself, or God, before you can move on.

Or are you more prone to resentment? Is there something that you recognize to be gnawing within you? Bring it to the Lord. Ask Him to help you express it, either just to Him (and yourself, of course), or to another person perhaps.

Thank you, Jesus, for wrestling all of our demons on our behalf on the cross. Help us to come to the cross and choose to surrender ourselves, thereby rendering our demons powerless and homeless, as they will no longer be able to dwell in our being.

Amen.

"Dance with Me" – Choosing Joy

It is difficult to believe that we have choices when we are in emotional pain, let alone see what they may be. I remember a difficult time in my own life such as this, where I was the person in pain. I became a member of a charismatic prayer group in 1977, and in 1978 through 1980 I was dealing with depression. And to top it off, there was the added burden of the guilt that I should not be depressed because I have received so much from the Lord. I was still very young (early 20's). But a broken engagement had sent me reeling for several years.

Often there are no words to comfort someone who is in a great deal of emotional pain or stress. I remember one evening after a prayer meeting, when my friend, who was the founder and leader of our prayer group, came up to me and asked me how I was doing. I just looked at her and told her I just could not get the sadness to lift – I felt like I was living under a heavy black cloud that would not give way to the "Sonshine."

We had shared in the past, and words had been lovingly offered and they helped a lot. But somehow that night she knew that words were not going to help. All of a sudden the man in the music ministry who played the fiddle, who happened to be her brother, started playing his fiddle. All by himself, not part of the prayer meeting music but just a lively tune that spontaneously came to him and he lifted his fiddle to play it while others were having coffee and chatting after the meeting. She looked at me and said "Dance with me!" I just looked at her, jolted out of our conversation thinking "What????" She said it again "Dance with me!" Then she took my hands and began to lead in what felt like a polka type of dance around the room where the prayer group had been. At first I felt clumsy and foolish and phony. The last thing I felt like doing was dancing. But then I felt the heaviness give way to a moment of joy that broke through like that Leonard Cohen song that says we all have cracks because that is how the light gets in. The light of joy got into a small crack that my dear friend had the wisdom to find.

I can see the Holy Spirit so much in that evening – inspiring my friend to come over to me, inspiring the fiddler with a joyful tune that he began to spontaneously play, and inspiring my friend to dare to take my hands and ask me to dance with her…and yes, even inspiring me to respond by daring to take new steps, and even twirl on the winds of joy. I do believe something changed in me that night, and healing happened in my broken heart.

Reflecting on this experience, the Lord showed me that I had to deliberately CHOOSE joy. And that it was there for me to choose.

What is joy? Scripturally, Paul teaches that joy is one of the fruits of the Holy Spirit (Galatians 5:22) – it is supposed to be an outgrowth of our spiritual life. Sometimes it helps to define something by stating what it is not. Recall a moment of joy in your life…it is not so much an emotion, or happiness or pleasure, but rather it is more like the ability to enjoy the moment as it is. Joy also has an element of surprise to it: - we can be surprised by joy. For me, an example of that is laughter. When I spontaneous give way to laughter it is a release of the Spirit. Can you recall a moment when you could not stop laughing! You really cannot recreate it and when you try to describe it to someone else, the words fall short, and it doesn't seem so funny. We say "you had to be there". So I think it isn't so much that something was so funny, but rather that in that moment I was somehow free to enjoy it!

Jesus says in Gospel John that He came that we might have life and have it in abundance (John 14). He says:

"Abide in Me so that My joy may be in you and that your joy may be full." or "complete." (John 15:11).

Our walk with Jesus is meant to be joyful. In the beginnings of the Charismatic Renewal, we were drowning in joy and we had no words to describe it. The gift of tongues gave us the ability to speak our joy, beyond words. Then we tried to capture the experience, and define it and worst of all, manage it! It became serious business rather than delighting in the Lord no matter what our life circumstances may have been at the time.

Other biblical references about joy are self-explanatory, and powerful:

"The joy of the Lord is my strength." (Isaiah 12:3).

"The Lord promises to turn our sorrow into joy (John 16:20) and

" God will give us the OIL OF JOY in exchange for the oil of mourning, and the garment of PRAISE for the spirit of heaviness" (Isaiah 61:3).

God knows we will deal with mourning and sorrow and heaviness and has provided the Spirit to give us joy.

Rejoice in the Lord always – no matter what your circumstances. Paul writes from prison – in there for 2 years before his execution when he writes this. "I count it all joy when I fall into various trials." (James 1:2)

Joy is like a well that we must draw from, God's Word to me is the joy and rejoicing of my heart! (Jeremiah 15:16) We need to remember to draw from the Word of God. It is an action verb, a choice to be made.

One way to draw from the well of joy is to LIVE IN THE PRESENT; if we are regretting the past, or fearing the future, we are not in the present where the Spirit is. We can only have joy NOW. We can remember a joyful moment, or anticipate one, but it can only be experienced in the present moment. Did you ever notice that the moment NOW is always ok? The grace is there... we are invited to **CHOOSE joy.**

Back to my friend's beautiful invitation to dance with her...I suspect that the Lord often tries to come to us this way...when we are praying, eyes cast down, or full of tears...when we are grieving, or feeling guilty, or after a beautiful time of heartfelt repentance, or after asking for help for ourselves or loved ones...when we feel vulnerable, alone or rejected...I can picture Him trying to catch our eyes so He can look lovingly into our soul and invite us to: "Dance with Me!"

He truly is the Lord of the Dance.

PRAYER

Recall a moment of joy that you experienced. It could be a moment of:

- Laughter that just springs up within you.

- Tears: tears of gratitude, love, repentance & forgiveness, of hearing or speaking truth.

- Joy when seeing beauty (e.g. a flower, the ocean, mountains in Vermont, a baby's perfect skin, a sunset or sunrise, fireworks...)

Get in touch with the experience of that moment of joy. Enjoy remembering it...

Try to stay in the moment now and experience that joy...

Imagine yourself drawing from the well of joy...see yourself walking up to it, looking at the empty bucket on the wall, taking it in your hands, dropping it down, and feeling yourself hoist up your joy.

Know that joy is within you, where the Spirit dwells. It is there to draw upon, at any time, at any moment, during any circumstance.

Imagine Jesus coming up to you and asking you to put down on the floor those things that are most deeply troubling you at this time in your life. Imagine Jesus lifting up your chin, so that His eyes can meet yours. Let Him lift your arms and hear His invitation "Dance with Me!"

Maybe you are not comfortable being intimate with Jesus... whatever the resistance, try to let it go and enter the dance with Jesus.

Let Him lead...maybe it will be a waltz, where He holds you and guides you gently. Or maybe it will be a polka, where He whisks you around playfully and helps you to let go of any heaviness. But whatever the dance, allow Him to take you to a new place of freedom and joy.

Thank you Jesus, for being my dance partner at this moment in my life with you.

Amen.

The Joy of a Correctable Mistake!

I made a mistake the other day. I was out to lunch with some friends and because I was the former engineer/math teacher, I was given the bill to calculate what we each owed. Simply put, I incorrectly calculated a tip for a waitress that was very kind, attentive, and well deserving of a great tip! Instead of giving her 20%, I accidentally miscalculated and left 10%.

Somehow, I discovered this error while asleep during the night. I woke up thinking of the way I calculated the tip and I woke up thinking "that can't be right!" It kept me tossing and turning (that's another story – how the Holy Spirit speaks to me in the middle of the night when something needs fixing, solving or answering…). Evidently it was important to the Lord as well as to me because I couldn't shake the nagging thought that I had short-changed her, and that she so deserved quite the opposite message.

I called the restaurant in the morning, wanting to provide my credit card number to give the waitress the rest of her tip – I tried to describe the waitress and the time of her shift, but long story short it was too complicated … so I drove back to the restaurant and luckily found the waitress that had served us yesterday. When I told her that I had made a mistake, and handed her the additional tip, she hugged me and said that I made her day. Not only that, but apparently I had done that and said nice words to her in front of her boss! So it was a double blessing for her!

This is worth a journal entry because most of my mistakes are not so easily undone – they usually have lingering consequences that cannot be reversed even when I say I am sorry and ask for forgiveness!

So I want to say Thank you Jesus for the experience of great joy to have made a correctable mistake!!! Not only was it correctable, but it gave the kind waitress a good moment as well that wouldn't have happened if I had done things right the first time.

I can't help but notice how this "happy" journal entry is so much shorter than my other ones! Perhaps I need to spend more time reflecting on how the Lord truly has redeemed many other mistakes I've made, maybe much more often than I realize, but in ways that may take a little longer to fix.

PRAYER

This prayer is a short verse, packed with infinite teaching and wisdom.

Ponder it for a while...

"All things work together for good to those who love God, who are called according to His plan and purpose." (Romans 8:28).

Amen.

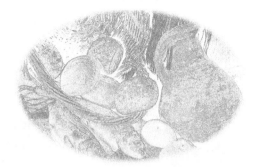

9

Walking on Water

There are many commentaries and books written about the powerful Gospel account in Matthew 14:22-33 when Jesus sent His disciples ahead of him to go via boat to "the other side" while He stayed behind to pray. After they set out, there was a storm at sea causing the disciples to panic in their boat. Jesus walks on the water to get to them in the midst of the storm, and when they see Jesus walking toward them they are even more frightened, thinking they were seeing a ghost. Jesus calls out to them "Fear not, it is I." Then Peter, in a moment of great faith and courage, cries out "Lord, if it is really You, then command me to come to You!" The Lord then commands Peter to step out of the boat and come to Him. As long as Peter is looking at Jesus, he can also walk on the water! But the moment he turns back and looks at the waves and the storm, he begins to sink. He cries out in fear "Lord save me!!!" Jesus immediately reaches for him and lifts him out of the sea onto the boat.

There are so many lessons in this short Gospel account. I would like to focus on Peter's first cry "Lord if it is really You!" and then the subsequent choice Peter made – that first step he took out of his boat onto the water.

There is a quote from Max Lucado that I love:

"Whether or not storms come, we cannot choose. But *where we stare* during a storm, that *we can.*"

I've heard sermons that teach us that when we choose to focus on our life's stormy circumstances, rather than on our faith and our relationship with Jesus, we will sink too. But if we choose to focus on Jesus, we too can walk on the water through our storms. I believe this to be true. It is also true that Jesus will never leave us and will always be there to reach out and lift us up.

I find myself drawn to Peter's spontaneous and faithful cry to Jesus – as if he was saying, Lord, empower me too! Considering the context of this gospel account, Jesus had just multiplied the loaves and the fish, using the contribution of a young boy and feeding thousands with his meager lunch. So I would imagine Peter's "faith meter" was particularly high after witnessing that. Peter is recognizing Jesus's authority over the natural, and the supernatural world begins to become a new reality. When Jesus walks on the water He is trumping all laws of nature and science – all of those laws are subject to Him. When Peter is focused on that reality where Jesus lives, he also has the power to transcend the natural. But when he looks back at the old reality – the storm, the waves, and his humanness – he sinks. What a powerful testimony to the authority of Jesus Christ, the Son of God and the Son of Man. And the fact that He can transfer His authority to a human being opens up a whole new meaning of being His disciple.

The first step that Peter took out of that boat is profound to me. Courage was required to actually put his faith into action. Peter may have succeeded for only a moment, but that was a great moment that he would never forget and would later grow from. The enemy to his complete success was fear. Just as it is our enemy. It is so sweet watching a toddler take their first step – and they are excited and proud of what they just did, even if they fall after 3 steps. That first step is the promise of many more to come.

I am reminded of the Exodus journey, when Yahweh parts the Red Sea for the Israelites to cross as they are fleeing Pharaoh's armies following Moses who is leading them out of Egypt. We get excited that God parts the sea, but can you imagine taking that first step onto the dry path in between two huge walls of water? Wouldn't you wonder how long it would last, and what might happen when you are halfway through? It is a similar challenge God offers us today... are you willing to take that first step into the unknown and unnatural place I am leading you to?

Most of us will never find ourselves in a boat being called to literally walk on the water, but what is the circumstance in your life at this moment where you sense the Holy Spirit might be calling you to step out of your boat – aka, your comfortable place that seemingly keeps you safe - and into a greater reality of His power and authority working through you in your life?

We are all in different life circumstances, but I think there is one common experience we can all relate to, and that is having the courage to speak our truth even when it is scary or uncomfortable or unpopular. There is the risk of being rejected, misunderstood, outnumbered, or mocked. I chose this focus because being called to speak our truth is not an age-dependent challenge – we are called to speak our truth throughout our entire lives. Consider these examples.

If you are a student in school, and you witness someone being bullied, it is a first step out of your boat to speak up to protect the person that is being bullied. At first the sound of your own voice speaking up for the sake of another may frighten you, but you will find that if you focus on Jesus and on His love for you and this other person, He will be there with you as you utter that first sentence and the Holy Spirit will give you the words to help you continue to speak. Speaking your truth can help set another person free.

PRAYER

Ask the Holy Spirit to show you a "boat" that you may be in…

It could be a situation that you are in that may be comfortable because it is familiar, but if you pay attention you see that it is not really comfortable, because you also feel constrained, limited, or confined?

Or perhaps it is a routine that you have outgrown and it may be becoming a drain on your enthusiasm for life, or for hope, or for courage to grow.

Do you sense the Lord's invitation to step out of or into something that will require more faith, and more trust in Him to accomplish?

Ask the Lord to show you.

Amen.

10

Needing to be Right vs. Being Right with God

I think I have a gift of being loyal, but as with any gift, there is an opposite side to it…a dark side if you will. When my loyalty goes too far, it becomes more like stubbornness. It is hard for me to admit that perhaps I am wrong, and I need to remind myself that it is good to revisit some of my answers to questions I have pondered. When I choose to fight to the death to defend my truth, rather than open my mind to dare to ask if I might be missing something, or worse… wrong, I am needing to be right rather than needing to be right with God.

It is not easy for any of us to find ourselves to be, well…wrong! Just plain wrong about something! We can be so sure, and then later learn something that we did not know. That light goes on and we realize we have leapt ahead with some assumptions that took us down a wrong path in our perceptions and our thinking. It became clear to me that I have to test the spirits…I have to discern everything to ensure not that I am right, but rather, that I am right with God. Because that is all that matters. And God gave us His Word to discern by.

Being right with God is when peace abounds. It doesn't mean that I am always perfect, but that I know that I am always perfectly loved by God, and invited into relationship with Him to grow more in understanding His ways and His wisdom. It means trusting God even when I cannot see His hand working in my life "for good, not evil, reserving a future full of hope for me." (Jeremiah 29:13). Being right with God may mean I don't have all the answers, and that I remain in that "cloud of unknowing" as I wait on God to reveal what He thinks I need to know, and when He thinks I can handle knowing more.

Being right is a good thing…I mean, who doesn't want to be right? But if the goal is to win an argument, or to prove that I am somehow superior to another, well then, that is useless. But if being right means that I have heard God's word spoken directly to me in a specific situation of my life, and that I am following God, then what I really mean is that I am right with God, not that I am right. We need to aspire to be right with God, allowing Him to show us through our relationship with Him *what* is right, and *what* is wrong; not so much *who* is right or *who* is wrong.

I can be right with God while still being wrong about a perception I may have or a conclusion I have drawn. Being right with God means He will continue to mold me, teach me, heal me and guide me into paths of righteousness. Sometimes being right with God means being able to say "I am sorry, I was wrong." The need to be right can be a sign of an arrogant personality.

Then there are those interesting times when I can be right, and so can you! I believe there are always three sides to every story, not two. There is my side, your side, and the truth (aka, God's side). Interesting indeed!

PRAYER

Invite the Holy Spirit into your prayer moment.

Recall a situation you are in now, or perhaps were in fairly recently, where you were in an argument or debate with someone over some issue. What is driving you within?

The desire or need to be right?

The need to win the argument?

The desire to see the other side?

Ask the Lord to help you see it through His eyes. Ask Him to speak to you and reveal His wisdom or give you a new insight into the impasse.

Did anything change?

Thank you Lord that You are present with me always, gently inviting me to:

"Ask and you shall receive, seek and you shall find, knock and it shall be opened unto you. For everyone who asks, receives; he/ she who seeks, finds; and he/she who knocks shall have the door opened unto him/her."

Amen.

PART II.

GOD WORKING THROUGH HUMANITY

Jacob's Son Joseph – Transformed by the Holy Spirit

Don't we often say, "if only this didn't happen to me, or if only I hadn't done that, or if only God didn't allow this…etc., then I would be really whole and free to be my true self and fulfill my purpose"? That can seem to be true, especially when we carry with us the consequences of our experiences. Yet, it is these very experiences that God uses to transform us when we surrender to His plan for our lives, and ask Jesus to be Lord of our lives. In Romans 8:28 we read that "All things work for good to those who love God, who are called according to His plan." That verse has brought me great comfort so many times in my life.

Transformation by the Holy Spirit is the process by which God molds us into who He created us to be, and who we long to become. We can see it at work in Joseph's journey in Genesis.

It is interesting to see that by working through the life of one man, Joseph, God is also working to accomplish His bigger plan to form His people Israel! It means that each one of our lives has a purpose for us, and also as part of the greater good. We are each a unique piece of God's wonderful plan.

Joseph is one of Jacob's twelve sons, his favorite son to be exact.

Joseph was also Rachel's son, who was the woman Jacob loved. Joseph was anointed by God at an early age with a special gift - the gift of having prophetic dreams and the ability to interpret those dreams which plays out in his destiny. Jacob gave Joseph a special gift – a beautiful multi-colored coat. In Genesis 37: 1-11 we find Joseph at 17 years old, having eleven brothers. He worked in the field as a shepherd boy, and one night he had a dream of his brothers bowing before him; and if that wasn't enough, then the sun and stars bowed to him as well! He made the big mistake of excitedly sharing this dream with his brothers. What older brothers want to hear a dream like this coming from the favorite little brother?!! Needless to say, Joseph's brothers were very jealous of him. Scripture says that they could not even wish him well. Given they were already jealous about the coat, can you imagine how hearing about this dream made them feel.

It is obvious that the brothers' sin was jealousy. But Joseph also has some culpability here – he had a lot of pride, self-esteem at best, and was also quite insensitive to the impact his father's favor had on his brothers. Even though he was anointed, he did not yet know how to live as God's anointed. This leads me to wonder how we interact with others at such times.

Joseph's eleven brothers plotted to kill him – think about that. All eleven of them are in agreement that this is the right thing to do! So they go out to work in the fields, and once far from their home, they first stripped him of his special coat, then they threw him into a deep well. Even though this literal stripping of his coat was significant and part of their plan (they planned to bring it home to their father Jacob as proof that Joseph was killed and likely eaten by a wild beast), I think there is also a spiritual significance to stripping him of his coat. That coat was a symbol of his special favor. Now he is naked. His brothers do not feel any remorse at all – they proceed to enjoy a meal and rejoice while he is in the bottom of the well, left to die.

Later they do have a change of heart because one brother, Judah, does not want Joseph's blood on their hands. So they decide to sell him as a slave, instead of leaving him at the bottom of the well to die. He was first sold to the Ishmaelites, then to Midianites then to the Egyptians, where he served Pharaoh's chief officer, Potiphar.

God continued to be with Joseph, just as He continues to be with each one of us during all of our circumstances. Joseph's time in slavery is one of hardship and longsuffering. In Genesis 39:7-12 we learn that Pharaoh's wife lusts for Joseph. He is handsome, gifted, and popular. She asks him to lie with her, and he faithfully says no because he would not dishonor Pharaoh, but even more importantly, he would not disobey God's law. Even now as a slave he would not even consider being in poor favor with God. Potiphar's wife takes his coat off of him as he is running away from her. She then falsely accuses him of trying to rape her, showing his coat. Isn't it ironic that he is again stripped of a coat? He is then thrown into prison.

Genesis 39: 20-23 continues to affirm that Joseph is still God's anointed one. The Lord was still with him. While in prison, Joseph is given the opportunity to use his gift of interpretation of dreams: he interprets the dreams of his fellow prison mates, the cupbearer and the baker. But this time he ACKNOWLEDGES that his ability is a gift from God, not of himself. This is the first time we see that Joseph has acquired a humility related to his giftedness. (Gen 40: 8) Just as Joseph prophesied, the cupbearer is freed, and the baker is hanged. Joseph asks the cupbearer to remember him, and to make known of his injustice (Genesis 40:14-15), but the cupbearer forgets Joseph (Genesis 40:23) once he is set free.

Two years later the cupbearer remembers Joseph's gift when Pharaoh needed an interpretation of a dream he had. Two YEARS LATER!!!!!!!!!! (Genesis 41:1) is a long time to wait!

We learn about Pharaoh's dream in Genesis 41:15-16. Joseph again states it is God who has the power to give the interpretation of the dream. He interprets the dream and also has the wisdom to provide a solution to the problem the dream warns about. What happens as a result of this is that Joseph is elevated even higher. Gen 41: 38 – 43, 46. Joseph was 30 years old.

The next step of Joseph's journey is that he is put into a position where he later ends up helping his father and brothers when a terrible famine strikes the land for 7 years. God saves Israel through Joseph. His dream from early childhood is then fulfilled when his brothers end up bowing before him, not recognizing him, when they went to Egypt seeking food from Pharaoh.

So, after many years, and much struggle, Joseph never loses his gifts from God but does learn humility. Pharaoh lifted him up to a position of leadership, and Joseph ends up with almost as much power and authority as the Pharaoh himself has. He is still God's anointed one, even in Egypt! (See Genesis 39 1-4 to read about Joseph's position of leadership).

Have you ever found yourself in a pit due to other's ill will, or your own pride? God does not abandon his anointed ones, ever. Even in the pit, and even in the pits of our own making.

There are so many insights that we can apply to our own faith journey when considering Joseph's journey. When God anoints a person, that anointing is not dependent upon circumstances. Sometimes God allows circumstances to happen. Sometimes those circumstances are consequences resulting from our own sinfulness and bad choices. Sometimes those circumstances are consequences of someone else's sin. Either way God is with us and uses those circumstances to transform us into God's anointed ones, chosen for a specific purpose, if we surrender to His will.

We see a change in Joseph after being in the well – he becomes humble. God allowed his brothers to do the evil they intended because God had a greater purpose. Joseph would never have gotten to Egypt to eventually save his family if they hadn't sold him as a slave. God also allowed Joseph to be imprisoned to further mold him. He was tested and he kept choosing to be right with God. Being in prison became an opportunity for Joseph to use and reveal his gift. We see the power of his gift increasing. Why did God allow Joseph to be imprisoned for so long; first due to his brothers' jealousy and cruelty, then later based on false accusation by Pharaoh's wife? I truly don't know, and God's sense of time is always very different than mine.

The other lesson I see is that Giftedness is not the same thing as Holiness. Joseph was always gifted. But through the circumstances of his journey he also became holy. That is when the power was used for God's glory, not for his own, and God's ultimate purpose for the people Israel could be fulfilled.

PRAYER

There is no compromise when choosing to be God's people. When we stand on Romans 8:28, and choose to be one of "those who love God, who are called in His plan," our lives must conform to God's will, not our own. God has a plan and He will work to accomplish it in us if we want Him to. The Israelites were constantly called to be set apart from the world, to do things God's way, not the way of the world or their own. They were not called to make sense out of things, but to have faith and trust and obey and use their gifts.

Where are you in your journey?

Are you in a pit? If you are not in a pit at all, thank God for that. Recall times you were in a pit and how God delivered you from it.

Thank God for that deliverance. Often we fail to thank God for the way "all things worked together for good." (Romans 8:28)

If you are in a pit due to consequences of your own mistakes, or your own sin, open your eyes to see that God is with you in your circumstance. Don't rationalize your choices; rather, own them and then ask for His forgiveness for whatever mistake you have made, and begin to praise and thank God that He has not abandoned you and that He will use even this wrongdoing for good in your life. Ask for His deliverance.

If you are in a prison due to someone else's ill will, open your eyes to see that God is with you. Try to forgive the person or persons who you feel have wronged you. Begin to praise and thank God that He has a plan for your life. Ask for His Justice and Truth to be revealed.

Amen.

Entering the Promised Land - Joshua

We are all searching for our Promised Land, and on this side of heaven, it always seems to elude us. We imagine what "perfect" looks like, and try to create that place, that scenario and those situations we imagine will bring us great joy. But sure enough, there is at least one thing that happens to unravel most, if not all, of our dreams. We just can't seem to recreate the bliss of the original Garden of Eden here on earth.

This should not be a surprise to us, because we truly are exiles here on planet Earth. We live in a place where the kingdom of God has come, and is yet to come. Because of Jesus, and the Holy Spirit within us, we can enter into prayer and thereby immediately enter into the Promised Land of peace beyond understanding, joy in the midst of sorrow, and justice in spite of injustice. God is with us while we live out our earthy lives.

God's kingdom on earth is found right where we stand when we stand in faith and pray in His name. His kingdom is also yet to come, and until Satan is judged and bound at the end of the world as we know it, the human race will continue to endure his constant merciless attacks on our efforts to get closer to the God. While we are exiled here on earth, we will always be journeying toward the Promised Land, without arriving there in all its fullness, until we pass from this world to the next.

It is helpful to understand our own spiritual journey by reflecting on Moses and the actual physical journey of the Israelites out of 400 years of slavery in Egypt into their possession of the Promised Land. God's manifestation of action to deliver of the Israelites began the moment Moses encountered the burning bush. I say manifestation because God's plan to answer the prayers of His people who were slaves and crying out for Him to help them was in motion long before Moses stumbled upon the burning bush. Moses was the first to behold the visible glory of God and to receive God's name: I AM. Moses was not perfect or holy – he had in fact just killed an Egyptian. But Moses was chosen, and made ready by God to begin the journey towards holiness through a personal relationship with God. This is a paramount revelation about the point of each of our journeys – the purpose is more about our relationship with God, rather than our destination.

God speaks through Moses, commanding Pharaoh to "Let My People Go!" He does not ask, he commands, and He prophesies warnings of the plagues that will fall on Egypt if Pharaoh does not comply. The plagues occur, one by one, confirming the truth and absolute authority of God's Word. God then leads the Israelites to and through the Red Sea, then drowns Pharaoh's army when it pursues the Israelites.

By the Lord's decree, His people are set free from slavery in Egypt, and are journeying in the desert. They are led by the Lord by a cloud during the day, and a pillar of fire by night. They are fed manna to prevent their starvation, and given water from a rock to quench their thirst. On a good day, Yahweh even provides quail for meat!

Even so, they struggled the same way we do now, even though

they were led by a visible sign of a cloud by day and a pillar of fire by night. Just like us they still doubted God's goodness and promise even after seeing signs and wonders. That tells us something...the problem isn't being able to see the cloud or knowing where God is leading, *the problem is in choosing to follow.* The Holy Spirit still leads us now - the cloud and the pillar of fire are now within our very hearts, nudging and guiding us by day and by night. We may be tempted to think "how good and easy they had it back then!" How easy it would be to follow the Lord if I could see a cloud by day, and a pillar of fire by night! But God still leads His people today through the same Holy Spirit that Jesus released to the Father from the cross when He declared "Father, into your hands I commend my Spirit."

The Father gave believers His very own Spirit at the Feast of Pentecost. We have the indwelling presence of the Holy Spirit, which is far more personal than a cloud or pillar of fire, to guide us. We have to listen for the whispers within our soul and mind and heart as the Spirit counsels "go this way, or beware of this trap." At times He may give us dreams that we sense have purpose and meaning, that when we reflect on them can give us a sense of direction. Or He speaks to us through others who also are following Him.

The journey of the Israelites out of Egypt and into the desert on route to the Promised Land is symbolic of our own spiritual journey. We are constantly called out of an Egypt, where we are in bondage and oppressed, not free, into a Promised Land that will be healthy and bring a new freedom from sin or woundedness. The blessing that is truly ours is that God is always with us on the journey, even when we don't feel His presence. God is with us through the parted Red Sea and He is with us in the desert. He shows us by their journey that He is there to sustain us by His real presence and provision, and will quench our thirst with Living Water.

It must have felt so awesome to be delivered from slavery, and so awesome to dwell in the midst of God's real presence! We say that about "them", but the same is true for us if we have spiritual eyes to see. We don't hear much about how happy they felt. It seems that, just like us, they hardly ever felt like they were anywhere near entering the Promised Land. We always have a gripe, don't we! And we yearn for more. We say we are not happy, and we mistakenly repeat the path of the Israelites by either looking back to old ways (aka idols) or searching for new idols to bring into the Promised Land with us. The irony is that each time we choose an idol, we lose the Way to the Promised Land, and return to wandering in the desert.

A second lesson in their journey can be found when the Israelites finally do arrive to the beginning of the land that God was giving them. They were on the verge of entering the land flowing with milk and honey, then Moses sent out twelve envoys to the Promised Land to scope it out. The people wondered "Is the land what God said it would be? Which really translates into the age old doubt: *"Is God who He says He is?"*

The twelve delegates enter and see that indeed this land is a luscious land, with clusters of grapes, pomegranates and figs - *they could see the fruits*. In Numbers 13:25-33, two of the twelve (Caleb - Judah, Joshua - Ephraim) saw and believed & trusted God. The other ten of the twelve made up a lie and came back and told the congregation that there were giants! They said "we were like grasshoppers next to them." Everyone became upset and fearful and turned on God again. They believed the lie of their fear rather than God's Word to them. It is amazing how quickly they, and we, the people of faith, put our trust in the words of people rather than choosing to stand on God's Word and the promises He offers us. We believe the words of people rather than the promises of God. *Why is it easier to trust the lie?* They rebelled and wanted to go back to Egypt.

Can you just hear the cry of the Father's heart in Numbers 14:11? "How long will My people not believe in Me?"

Again Moses intercedes for his people, so they would not be destroyed by God. God does not destroy them but declares that their generation would not enter the Promised Land. Perhaps they never entered the Promised Land because they chose not to.

Numbers 14:20-24 tells us that only Caleb and Joshua will enter the Promised Land. Caleb has a different Spirit. He sees SPIRITU-ALLY. In God's words, "He follows Me completely." We learn that is how we become able to enter the Promised Land.

Our challenge is to stay on track on our way to the Promised Land without turning back to Egypt. Why do we remember Egypt so fondly? It reminds me of what psychiatrists call the "Stockholm Syndrome" – which describes the hostage mentality - when hostages are kept for a long time, they find a way to adjust to captivity and actually develop a fear of being released. They become more comfortable with old bondage than new freedom. The devil we know is more comfortable than the unknown experience of living free as a child of God in His kingdom.

We are all somewhere on a personal journey from an Egypt that at one time enslaved us, going through a desert that is meant to purify us, on our way to a Promised Land that will finally fulfill us.

What is the Promised Land? Our feeble and limited vision of it is probably about as vague as the Scriptural description of a "land that is flowing with milk & honey." When I was a child I asked my father what heaven would be like – he said there would be mountains of ice cream that never melt! And we all have a spoon! My current adult vision vs. God's vision must be just as limited. ***Do we believe in the Promised Land? Or even more unsettling…do we believe that we will like it there? That it is good?*** Are we looking forward to getting there?

From God's perspective, the Promised Land is the place where God will dwell with humankind, and in God's words, ***"YOU SHALL BE MY PEOPLE AND I SHALL BE YOUR GOD." Leviticus 26:11-12***

It is much more about our relationship with God than about the land we live on. God wanted them to occupy the land--to take ownership of it. To establish a nation where "You shall be My people and I shall be your God."

There is another lesson to learn from the Israelite's journey – timing matters as well as the direction we are headed. We have to GO AT GOD'S BIDDING. The Israelites arrive at the edge of the land they are to possess, but they have grossly sinned on their way. They acknowledge that they have sinned but do not repent. Moses warns them "God is not among you - you will be killed." The 10 delegates decide to enter the land anyway. They do not listen and they do not RESTORE their relationship with God first. Rather, they presumptuously go into the Promised Land without God, without the Ark of the Covenant, and without Moses, God's anointed and appointed leader over them...and they perish. We cannot go without God! As Jesus says in John "I am the vine and you are the branches. Apart from Me you can do nothing."

We must go at God's bidding, and allow God to establish His kingdom through us, not the other way around. I used to say with lots of enthusiasm and bright ideas "Here I am Lord, follow me!" Now with a little less enthusiasm but a lot more conviction, I say "Here I am Lord - I haven't a clue how to do Your will, please lead me."

The Kingdom of God, heaven, is both here and now as well as yet to come. When we see with spiritual eyes, we understand our command to take the Promised Land by force as a spiritual battle; a call to overcome the kingdom of evil by establishing the kingdom of God wherever we are. Our battle is "Not against flesh & blood but against principalities of darkness" Ephesians. *It is a spiritual battle.* It has been said that if you do not know you are in a spiritual battle then you are probably losing the battle! We need to fight, which for Christians really means, we need to care. Caring is the opposite of apathy. We need to choose to uphold TRUTH when it is uncomfortable and unpopular, to call for JUSTICE when it might cost us something to do so.

Moses was not spared the journey either and ultimately he was not allowed to enter the Promised Land either because he struck the rock (as God had asked him to do before) rather than obey the new command to instead "speak to the rock." God was angry that he didn't obey the <u>new</u> word but *rather relied on what worked before.* As if his power was in how hard he could strike the rock! No. The power was in his obedience to God's word, and belief that God would work through him. Like us, Moses began to believe in the action he took before, and in his own performance of that action, rather than believing in God's Word given in the moment "now."

At first and for years this troubled me greatly – I mean, if Moses could mess up and not be allowed to enter the Promised Land, what hope is there for me? But when you understand that the Promised Land is the place where God says "you are Mine and I will be your God," when you really think about it, there was nothing in the Promised Land that Moses did not have already on his mountaintop overlooking the land. Moses had seen God face to face and dialogued with Him regularly. Scripture records that Moses's face would shine with the Glory of God after a prayertime! God's kingdom had already been established in Moses. In some ways God spared him further journey because he was already there. Could it be that He brought Moses to a mountaintop to spend the rest of his days there in peace, rather than as a punishment to not enter the Promised Land with the others? Here are God's own words about His servant Moses:

Numbers 12:68 (NIV) "Listen to my words: "When a prophet of the LORD is among you, I reveal myself to him in visions, I speak to him in dreams. {7} But this is not true of my servant Moses; he is faithful in all My house. {8} With him I speak face to face, clearly and not in riddles; he sees the form of the LORD. Why then were you not afraid to speak against my servant Moses?"

PRAYER

Consider your own spiritual journey, similar to the Israelites journey. Define Egypt as a place where you were not free, where you were in bondage, where you were limited by the powers that be, or by your own fear.

Can you recall an Egypt that God called you out of? Did God lead you to freedom? If so, how did He lead you?

Is there an Egypt in your life now that God is calling you out of? If you are presently in an Egypt, ask God to help you hear Him call you out of this Egypt and out of your fear to leave it behind.

Are you wandering in the desert? You sense that you followed the call to come out of Egypt but you have not yet entered the Promised Land? What is the Promised Land to which you are being called? Ask the Lord to help you rely on Him; to help you see the cloud by day and the pillar of fire by night.

What are the giants that keep you from entering this land? Giants such as:

Fear of failure, fear of confrontation, tradition, apathy, pride, logic, lack of faith or belief in God, embarrassment, anger, or closed doors?

Remember that the notion of giants is a fear, based on lies. What are the fears that appear to be giants in your Promised Land? What might be the lie underlying your fear that you are believing rather than trusting in God?

Lord I give you my life and my journey.

Help me to be content with the manna that you provide to sustain me and not long for Egypt which I falsely remember as bringing me fulfillment. I forget how enslaved I was.

Help me to enter the Promised Land in my life that you have called me to inherit - to establish your kingdom wherever you lead me, and not to imagine giants so that I never receive life in abundance.

Help me to keep going forward without turning back.

Lord, help me to become a Giant of Faith in your kingdom and for your kingdom. Help me to believe in You in a gigantic way!

Refresh me Lord with Your presence - with Your love, Your healing and forgiveness and the empowerment and gifts of the Holy Spirit.

I ask this through Jesus Christ my Lord,

Amen.

3

The Heart of David

Scripture says that David was a man after God's own heart (Acts 13:22). What does it mean to have a heart like God's? By looking at key accounts of David's life, throughout his entire lifetime, we can get a sense of his heart.

When the prophet Samuel obediently went to David's father's house to anoint the future king of Israel, he did not know who exactly he would be anointing. He just knew the name of the father of that future king, and where he lived. Samuel brought his flask of anointing oil and entered the home of Jesse (1 Samuel 16). Jesse proudly parades seven of his sons to Samuel, while Samuel looks, prays, and shakes his head "no…not this one." When seven of Jesse's sons had been introduced, and dismissed, Samuel asks if there is any other son. Well, it turns out that there is! David, a very young shepherd boy, who is out tending the sheep. Samuel asks to see David. Surely it cannot be that son! But Scripture (1 Samuel 16:7) tells us that "God sees differently than how man sees." When David is brought to Samuel, the light of the Holy Spirit lights upon Samuel and he exclaims "this is the chosen one." God sees as man does not. The least is the greatest. At this point, scripture shows us that the heart of David is that of a shepherd boy.

Later we find an adolescent (?) David watching the dreaded army of the Philistine's attacking Israel's army – God's people. Among their enemy is a giant…a very large and aggressive murderous man who is asking if the army of Israel has even one volunteer to fight with him. Kind of like "give me your best…give me what you've got!" There was great fear in the hearts of the Israelites, except for one heart, David's. The spirit of fear could not wrap itself around David's heart. His heart was fearless, because he was full of faith and trust in a God who was bigger than anyone in all of creation, even this giant. So he volunteered to fight the Philistine the same way he fought the lions and wolves that would try to devour his sheep. So, in addition to a shepherd's heart, we now see a fearless heart, one that has perfect faith in God. King Saul first tries to talk him out of taking on the fight, but to no avail. David volunteers to fight the giant…to be that one from all of Israel's army. King Saul is not comfortable with that, protecting young David, but David is persistent and not afraid. King Saul then gives David his own armor to wear. David tries it on and finds it is too cumbersome. This is symbolic to me, in that David's strength comes from the faith in his heart, not in King Saul's armor. He chooses his everyday tool – his slingshot – and instantly delivers a fatal blow to the Philistine – one stone to the head. No big bloody war, just a perfectly placed stone directed by the Lord's hand through David's faith. God saved His people through one faithful heart.

Much later in Scripture, when David is no longer a child, we see King Saul seeking to kill David because David has become a threat to his kingship (similar to the way King Herod wanted to kill the Jesus at His birth, because it was prophesied that He would be Israel's king). David found and entered King Saul's camp undetected, and got so close to King Saul while Saul was heavily asleep that he was able to take his sword. David chose not to kill Saul because of his loyalty to God's anointed king. Interestingly, David respected the authority of King Saul, whom God had previously anointed. There is a lesson here about respecting God's anointing, and the irrevocable Word of God when it is pronounced over a person's life. David put aside the glory of becoming king, preferring to wait for God's timing to reveal itself. The heart of David was again faithful to God's will and to a Word and a desire more important than his own. This is reminiscent of the heart of Jesus in the Garden of Gethsemane when He prays "Father, not my will but thy will be done."

David's life story takes a different turn when he meets Bathsheba, the beautiful wife of one of David's soldiers. She captivated him. He committed adultery and murder in order to take her as his wife. Here we see a lustful heart, a part of David that is not yet converted, nor holy. But God remains faithful to His spoken Word and anointing upon David, and it is interesting to see that just as David respected King Saul's authority, and did not kill him when he had the opportunity, God too continued to uphold his anointing on His servant David, even in David's sinfulness. The Lord sends Nathan the prophet to David, who speaks the truth to him of what he has done in God's eyes, and calls him to repentance. It is then that we see David's heart transform into a repentant heart.

Scripture shows us that David had a shepherd's heart, a fearless heart, a loyal and faithful heart, a lustful heart, and a repentant heart. Above all, he had a heart that loved God above all else. It is good for us to see that God remained pleased with David because of his great love for God. God could work with David, because David had a genuine love, holy fear of the Lord, and a respect and obedience to God's authority and ways. It gives us hope as sinners that a heart that truly loves God and chooses to acknowledge and repent of sin when it is realized, will be forgiven. This is the person that God says is "the man after God's own heart."

PRAYER

Lord, You created each one of us and gave us a name known only to You. You have assigned each of us a specific destiny; some great, like King David was called to, and some seemingly small. None of us can measure what is small or great in Your great plan and purpose for our lives. We don't know how we fit together, or how great a simple choice we make can be for the sake of others we do not even know.

What You need from us isn't our perfection or our greatness. What You need from us is:

- Our response of love of You,

- Our acknowledgment and repentance when we fail,

- Faith that believes that Your ways are greater than our ways, that Your will is more perfect than our will, and that Your motives are always for good.

Lord, thank you for the gift of my life. Thank you for my God-given destiny. Soften my heart so that I seek to grow closer to You, no matter how imperfect it may be at this moment in time. Holy Spirit, give me the grace to nurture my heart for God and His ways.

In the Name of Jesus,

Amen.

4

Condemnation vs. Conviction – The Woman at the Well

I've often heard the gospel about Jesus's encounter with a Samaritan woman at the well where she came to draw water. (John 4:4-42). Jesus asks her for a drink, which is remarkable because a Jewish man would not be talking to a Samaritan woman. She asks Him about this, and He replies that if she knew who He was, asking her for a drink, she would instead be asking Him for a drink! The woman moves from the initial literal understanding of the conversation, to realizing that Jesus was the Messiah, source of ever flowing Living Water. This transformation happens when Jesus shows His intimate knowledge of her by telling her everything she had ever done. Somehow, His knowledge of her life, and of her personhood, converts her to not only follow Him, but evangelize her entire town and introduce Him to others, who come to believe in Him on their own encounter.

To be honest, I find it baffling that when Jesus "told the woman everything she had ever done" her reaction was complete joy! That is hardly the reaction most of us would have when hearing about the mistakes of our life!

So there must be something new and different here…some good news to be realized.

When Jesus showed her, and now us our sin, it is a liberation, not a judgment. Allow me to digress...I am reminded of a person who works out in nature with wildlife and for example finds a beautiful hawk that has been caught in the netting of some plastic debris. The nature person has to find a tool to gently cut the netting without frightening the animal too much, with the goal of setting the bird free. A judgment would be something like "stupid bird, how did you ever get caught in this net."

When we pray and hear a voice that causes us to feel ashamed, guilty, more afraid, and more stuck in a bad set of circumstances, it is not the voice of God. When the Lord speaks to us, even about our sins, He is still loving and the sound of His voice and His words bring us peace and freedom. We get a flash of insight, seeing ourselves through His eyes and perspective, and we see that we are indeed caught. And He always invites us out of our mistakes.

The woman at the well rejoiced that this prophet of God, which is who she understood Jesus to be at first, actually and really knew her! Someone she had never met before knew the details of her life – sin as well as the associated sorrow that accompanies sin after the temptation fades and leaves us often with unbearable, certainly unwanted, consequences. But there is such joy that comes from being really seen and known, and still respected. That is the tenderness of our God towards us. Somehow she chooses to follow Jesus and becomes an evangelist that gets her entire town to hear Him and believe in Him. Her inviting words were simply "Come and meet this prophet – He told me everything I ever did!"

Perhaps the easiest way to understand the difference between condemnation and conviction is the motive. One causes a person to walk away liberated, empowered to make a healthy life-giving next choice. The other causes us shame and guilt, and offers no way out.

Jesus always offers a way out of our sin…He is the Way.

PRAYER

Does the thought of sitting quietly to meet Jesus in prayer and talk about YOURSELF bring you fear or comfort?

Do you feel like hiding or rehearsing your words, or do you feel like talking freely and pouring out to Him?

Jesus invites you to come to Him and pour out your heart. He wants to listen, just to you.

Allow Him to help you sift out what is good and what is harmful.

He knows where you are, He knows where you have been, and He knows the path that He can offer to you at this point in time. It is a path that He will not only show you, but will also walk beside you on.

Let Him show you how He sees you.

Amen.

Following Peter from Gospels to Acts

Peter is above all, our beloved brother in Christ. I know…he was a disciple, an apostle, our first Pope, and now a confirmed saint in the Catholic Church. But above all, Peter is a man who upon meeting Jesus, chose to follow Him, giving up everything. He had a conversion, just as we can, and chose to follow Jesus even to his own death on a cross. He was crucified upside down because he did not feel worthy to die the same way as His Lord. Because there is much written in the bible about Peter, and even by Peter, we can look at his life, his journey, his transformation to gain insight into our own journey following Jesus.

Recall the following gospel accounts about Simon (later renamed Peter by Jesus):

- Peter was a fisherman by trade. When Jesus met him He told Peter He would make him a fisher of men. (Matthew 4:19, Mark 1:17)

- Matthew 14:22 Peter walks on water as long as he continues to look at Jesus

- Matthew 16:13-19 Jesus asks the disciples "Who do you say that I am? Only Simon answered "You are the Christ, the Son of the Living God." Jesus then renames him "Peter", which means the Rock, and tells him that He will build His church upon "this rock."

- Matthew 16:21-23 Peter tries to stop Jesus from going to Jerusalem where He will be killed; Jesus responds "Get thee behind Me Satan."

- Matthew 17:1-8 Peter was one of three disciples that witnessed Jesus' transfiguration

- Matthew 26: 69-75 Peter denied 3 times even knowing Jesus before the cock crowed twice, just as Jesus prophesied.

- John 21: Jesus asks Peter 3 times if he loves Him, which troubled Peter because he felt Jesus was doubting his love, but Jesus was brilliantly setting Peter free from his 3 denials. Jesus asks "Peter, do you love Me? Feed My sheep..."

Peter's journey is further told, and in even greater detail, in the Book of Acts. We are much more familiar with Peter in the Gospels – partly because we hear the gospels read at church much more often than we read the Book of Acts of the Apostles. For this reflection, I want to move with Peter into the Book of Acts so we can see the change in him after he encountered the Risen Christ, and the Holy Spirit at Pentecost. He, and his life, changed dramatically.

Now let's follow Peter to the Book of Acts:

- Acts 1:15-26: Peter selected a replacement for Judas (gift of leadership)

- Acts 2: 1-41: Peter explained the Holy Spirit's coming at Pentecost (gifts of preaching, wisdom and understanding) – **Acts 2:39 – promise is for you & your children**

- Acts 3: 1-11: He healed a lame man from birth who was 40+ years old when the man was begging. Peter said "Silver nor gold have I none, but what I have I will give to thee...in the name of Jesus of Nazareth, rise up and walk!" Peter explains to amazed people that it was Jesus, not him, who healed the man, which demonstrated that Jesus was still alive (gift of healing).

- Acts 4:3: Peter and John get arrested for healing the man and preaching about Jesus,

- Acts 4:13: people were amazed at Peter's confidence and wisdom because they knew he was uneducated and untrained... just a simple fisherman...

- Acts 4:16-20: they let Peter and John go, charging them not to preach anymore; they say we cannot stop speaking what we have seen and heard

- Acts 4:29-31: Peter prayed for confidence in spite of threats, and received power

- Acts 5:1-11: Pronounces judgment on Ananias and Sapphira for lying to the Holy Spirit about their possessions that were at that time being assessed – they died as Peter prophesied would happen to them shortly (gift of prophecy).

- Acts 5:14-16: Many are healed by Peter, even those standing in a crowd as Peter's shadow touched them.

- Acts 5:17-20: Peter is imprisoned by high priest/released by angel of the Lord who opened gates and said "go your way and speak to the people in the temple" - they went and continued to preach in the temple!

- Released from prison in Acts 12:1-17. An angel said "get up and go...you are free..." Peter thought he was dreaming but just kept walking. Demonstrates his gift of working miracles.

- Acts 5:29: Peter says "we must obey God rather than men." This to me is the statement about his unwavering obedience to Jesus's call on his life, and his love for Jesus. Compare this to the 3 denials in the gospels and you see the transformation in Peter.

- Acts 9:32-42: healed Aeneas who was paralyzed for 8 years and raises Dorcas from the dead. Demonstrates his gift of healing.

- Acts 10: God calls Peter out of his comfort zone. God gives him a dream where he is told to eat unclean food. This upset Peter as it went against his traditional Jewish religious doctrine. In parallel God gave a dream to a man named Cornelius, a Gentile, telling him about Peter. Cornelius sends for Peter and Peter goes to him, enters his home and eats the food set before him. This again shows the depth of his obedience to the "now word" from the Holy Spirit, even when it went against his religious beliefs. Though St Paul was more called to preach to the Gentiles, while Peter remained preaching to the Jews, he was also sent to the Gentiles.

When Peter walks on the water in Matthew 14:22-32 in the gospels, we see the human side of Peter, with his occasional moments of faith and commitment to Jesus. In Acts we see him inflamed with the Holy Spirit, cooperating with the Holy Spirit. Peter goes from disciple to apostle. **And his ministry looks an awful lot like Jesus' ministry**.

Which Peter do you most identify with…Peter in the gospels or Peter in Acts?

It is interesting to me that people are not drawn to religion, but rather to people that are empowered by the Holy Spirit, who try to walk in the footsteps of Jesus. Crowds flocked to Jesus and to the apostles in Acts.

The world, as well as the church, are so hungry for the power of the Holy Spirit. The world, and unfortunately the church too, seek this power in wrong places – counterfeits of the spiritual gifts. We look for heroes in the absence of true apostolic leadership; we hunger for prophecy (e.g. for God to tell us what is happening and to reveal what will happen) but rather than seeking God, they seek mediums (King Saul did this and perished); we want healing so we seek Yoga and Chakras and crystals and "Mother Earth" and other "New Age" spirituality – this is not "new" at all but very "Old Age" - rather than seeking more of the Holy Spirit. The Israelites fell into this sin all the time. King Solomon failed God by turning ever so slowly to pagan gods that his wives worshiped.

We fall for the lie that God is boring, that we are to follow religion blindly, or that we know all there is to know about God's way. This is very dangerous spiritually, because it pulls us outside of God's covering over us. The lie whispered to us is "try something new!" when it is really not new at all, but Satan wearing a different cloak. When we freely choose to tamper with other spirituality outside of God's provision, we are not safe anymore. God will respect our free will and our choice to leave His side. There is so much to find when we choose to seek more of the power of the Holy Spirit; there is so much untapped power that has been given to us, and is meant to be flowing through us. But Satan keeps us away from our power heritage. We have such limited time while here on earth, let's not waste it by seeking the thrill of power and excitement outside of the Holy Spirit.

How do we grow more in the power of the Holy Spirit?

The answer is found in Acts 5:29, spoken by Peter:

"We must obey God rather than men."

PRAYER

Holy Spirit, I invite you to come into my life.

I ask you to release the gifts that God has placed in me; gifts that have been chosen to set me free to be the person I was created to be, to fulfill the purpose I sense is within me; gifts that will empower me to spend my time and energy working on things I am passionate about.

Show me the desires you have placed in my heart that you want to fulfill. Show me my purpose here on earth.

Release in me the gifts of your Spirit that I need so I can serve you beyond my own human limitations.

St. Peter, pray for me to surrender to the beautiful freedom of obedience to God's call, not to what people want me to do or not do.

Amen.

6

The Church as the Bride of Christ

There are several images of the church, and even more perceptions of what the church of Jesus Christ is supposed to be today. This reflection focuses on the image of the church as the Bride of Christ. I find it interesting that the image given to us in Scripture is not Jesus and His Wife, but rather Jesus and His Bride. I believe God is trying to find the symbol that will most capture the reality of our union with Christ – its joy, its purity, its fullness of love beyond all measure; the way the bride and groom see each other and feel for each other on their wedding day is an insight into how God envisioned the Church to be in relation to Him.

We can all recall being struck by the beauty of a bride coming down the aisle to meet her groom…she is her absolute best self, and her garments are clean, sparkling with majesty and fine material. Loved ones contribute to making the bride's ensemble complete – from borrowed and blue, to gifts of jewelry to wear on this special day. This didn't just happen – it took much planning and searching for "what will make it perfect" to create this moment – to be our best self for our beloved.

And then there is the groom waiting to receive this bride…looking at photos from many weddings, the look on the bridegroom's face is one of awe, appreciating how amazingly beautiful is this beloved woman he has chosen to be his wife.

It is important to note that the image of a bride is not meant to be a sexual image. In the same way that we learn to interpret the word "brethren" as encompassing all believers in Jesus Christ, so too we need to interpret the word "bride" as encompassing all believers in Jesus Christ. "Bride" describes our position of honor in relation to Jesus, which is meant to symbolize how beloved we are to Christ, and how pure and beautiful He has made us.

The Bride and Bridegroom then celebrate their love and new union with a feast and great joy. The love between the Bride and the Bridegroom is prophetic of our eternal future as well as of our finite time on earth. We are told in Scripture that Jesus is the Bridegroom, and we believers are the Bride. We are also told that Jesus will come again for His Church, His Bride, when she is ready. So the times we live in are the times to prepare. How do we prepare? Preparation begins first and foremost by responding to Jesus's love for us by loving Him in return. We need to "fall in love with Jesus", who already is head over heels in love with us. Our marriage vow goes beyond "until death do us part", as it will culminate in eternal life with Jesus.

The first place in the New Testament that we hear about the image of bride and bridegroom as the symbol of our relationship to Jesus is spoken by John the Baptist in Gospel John:

> John 3:28-30 (NIV) "You yourselves can testify that I said, 'I am not the Christ but am sent ahead of him. The bride belongs to the bridegroom. The friend who attends the bridegroom waits and listens for him, and is full of joy when he hears the bridegroom's voice. That joy is mine, and it is now complete. He must become greater; I must become less.'"

The second time is in the Book of Revelations where the church is described as being prepared as a bride, symbolizing the New Jerusalem:

Revelation 21:1-5 (NIV). "Then I saw a new heaven and a new earth, for the first heaven and the first earth had passed away, and there was no longer any sea. [2] I saw the Holy City, the New Jerusalem, coming down out of heaven from God, prepared as a bride beautifully dressed for her husband. [3] And I heard a loud voice from the throne saying, 'Now the dwelling of God is with men, and he will live with them. They will be his people, and God himself will be with them and be their God. [4] He will wipe every tear from their eyes. There will be no more death or mourning or crying or pain, for the old order of things has passed away.' [5] He who was seated on the throne said, 'I am making everything new!' Then he said, 'Write this down, for these words are trustworthy and true.'"

Then again in verses 9-11:

"One of the seven angels who had the seven bowls full of the seven last plagues came and said to me, 'Come, I will show you the bride, the wife of the Lamb.' [10] And he carried me away in the Spirit to a mountain great and high, and showed me the Holy City, Jerusalem, coming down out of heaven from God. [11] It shone with the glory of God, and its brilliance was like that of a very precious jewel, like a jasper, clear as crystal..."

So if marriage is our ultimate union with God, when Jesus returns for us, His Bride, we are now more like in a period of betrothal. We have made a commitment, but we are still free to choose. It is both a time of preparation and of waiting.

In 2 Corinthians St. Paul expresses concern about the Body of Christ, and poses the question: Will we be faithful until the bridegroom returns?

2 Corinthians 11:23 (NIV). "I am jealous for you with a godly jealousy. I promised you to one husband, to Christ, so

that I might present you as a pure virgin to him. [3] But I am afraid that just as Eve was deceived by the serpent's cunning, your minds may somehow be led astray from your sincere and pure devotion to Christ. "

This image of Adam and Eve is symbolic in that Jesus is the new Adam, and the church is the new Eve. In Genesis, as God opened Adam's side to pull out a rib and create Eve, Jesus was lanced in His side on the cross, from which the church was born. Just as Eve had a choice to listen to the serpent's deceptive promise to eat and become her own God, we the church still have that same choice. Do we choose to believe that God's Word to us is true? Or do we eat of the forbidden tree?

We often hear that "Jesus paid the price." Taken at face value, what do these words mean? What is the "price", and who gets "paid"? Perhaps we can find deeper understanding by looking at the Hebrew tradition of engagement and marriage. Prior to engagement, the groom asks the father of the bride for his daughter's hand in marriage, and they negotiate a price that must be paid by the groom to the bride's father. If they agree then they seal it with a cup of wine. The bridegroom then goes off to prepare a place for his future bride in his father's household. We hear this in the words "A man shall leave his mother and a woman leaves her home, they shall travel on to where the two shall be as one", which became a popular wedding song written by Paul Stookey.

Jesus, our Bridegroom, paid the price for us with His blood, giving His life for us on the cross. After original sin, Satan, the father of lies, took ownership of the world that Adam and Eve gave to him by disobeying God and following him. He is an evil father, "owning us," and keeping us imprisoned here on planet earth, the "world." Jesus' death on the cross was the price He paid for the bride He loved and rescued, and He brings her home to live in His Father's house.

The question for the time we are in here on earth is...Will we remain faithful until the Bridegroom returns?

PRAYER

Let us make a conscious acceptance of our betrothal to Jesus. We do this by accepting His death on the cross for each of us personally.

Now in this time of preparation, a time of cleansing & purification, we seek to make choices that keep us faithful to our betrothal. In Ephesians 5: 25 - 28 we hear that Christ loved the church and gave Himself up for her, to make her holy, cleansing her by the washing with water through the Word, and to present her to Himself as a radiant Church, without stain or wrinkle or any other blemish, but holy and blameless.

See yourself getting ready, as a bride adorns herself for the groom.

See yourself as beautiful, without spot or blemish.

Imagine the bridegroom coming for you - see His eyes, His joy, His love, His desire to be united.

Vows: We the church, take you Jesus, to be our lawfully wedded husband.

We promise to be true to you,

In good times and in bad,

For richer or for poorer,

In sickness and in health

Until death...when our union will finally be perfect and complete.

Revelation 19:79 (NIV). "Let us rejoice and be glad and give him glory! For the wedding of the Lamb has come, and his bride has made herself ready. [8] Fine linen, bright and clean, was given her to wear. [Fine linen stands for the righteous acts of the saints.] [9] Then the angel said to me, 'Write: **"Blessed are those who are invited to the wedding supper of the Lamb!"**'And he added, 'These are the true words of God.'"

Let the joy that is set before us give us courage to persevere through this time of purification!

Amen.

On Being Disciples

We often use the word "Disciple" interchangeably with "Apostle" I recall when I first read the gospels and noticed Jesus had many disciples, but only 12 apostles (13 if you count St. Paul who became an apostle after Jesus's resurrection.) So what is a disciple and how is that different than being an apostle?

A disciple is one who <u>follows</u> – Jesus called out to many "Follow Me." Apostles are assigned a mission. Disciples could become Apostles, but not all disciples are apostles. The focus of this reflection is on being disciples…more specifically, being Jesus's disciples…one who has chosen to follow Jesus.

I heard a quote on the radio: "When we are in step with the Lord, we are often out of step with the world." That caught me because it reminded me of when Jesus said to his disciples "the world will hate you because it first hated Me." (John 15:18) That raised two questions for me; first, *why* does the world hate Jesus? Then…gee, do I really want to walk that path? With my fragile sense of self-worth and need to be liked and accepted, this promises to be a painful journey.

Why do we follow Jesus? Why do YOU follow Jesus? Why do I follow Jesus? We need to answer that question for ourselves. It is central to everything, particularly our witness. Jesus posed a similar question to His twelve disciples when they were struggling with His teachings and after many of the other disciples decided to turn away and no longer follow Him. Jesus asks them "will you also leave?" And there was a silence… I'm sure quite a measurable one at that, before Peter replies "To whom else shall we go? You have the words of eternal life." (John 6:68). That realization is ultimately the bare-bones motivation and inspiration to continue to follow Jesus. I think that we do not doubt that we love Jesus, but something in us knows that the journey of following Him will cost us a lot…and at times cause us to be out of step with the world, and loved ones. And when Jesus Himself told the apostles that the world will hate us because it first hated Him, we fear the cost may be more than we can handle. I also believe that if we choose to follow Him because we love Him, and we really have come to know that He is the Way, the Truth and the Life, we can never turn away from Him, even when there are moments of doubt and fear. However, if we are only following Him out of fear, or routine, or a faith that was handed down to us that we never really chose for ourselves, then we may easily choose to turn away like many did.

Following Jesus out of fear does not provide a solid path to walk on. As we reflected in Part I, Chapter 3 on "Dealing with Fear," at the base of our fear is a lie. If our inner thoughts and belief is "if I don't follow Jesus, then God will 'get me', so I'd better follow Him", then we are believing a lie and succumbing to fear. When we choose to follow a different way, away from Him, or prefer not to listen to the truth, there are inevitable consequences to that choice because Jesus really IS who He says He is. So it is not a matter of God being "out to get us" – we suffer because we have opted to escape the safety of His way, and we are vulnerable to the consequences of sin. When Jesus tells us in John 14:6 that He is the Way the Truth and the Life, He is showing us the path that leads to joy, peace, happiness, salvation, and eternal life. Other paths lead elsewhere – we don't need to list all the "elsewheres" – but suffice it to say that is where the pain of sin is found.

If we follow Jesus out of routine, or because our parents did, or because our peers do, or for any other reasons that have nothing to do with our own free will, then we find ourselves walking on a path that is not solid. Why? Because it is not solidly *our own* path. We have to make it our own by making our own choices, not by inheriting or adopting or accepting the choices that others have made.

When I choose to follow Jesus by my faith in Him, because I believe He really is the Way – the ONLY way! and that His words are really TRUTH – the ONLY TRUTH! and that He is the LIFE – eternal life! then I am following Him with an undivided mind, heart, soul and strength. That is when I will find the joy in following Him, and when I could never even consider turning away from Him. When I am walking on that solid path of my true faith in Him, it is then that my life and its purpose are fulfilled, which has the consequence of true joy, peace and happiness at the deepest level of my being, so fulfilled that I may no longer even notice that the world has hated me along the way!

Another blessing of being a follower of Jesus is that, as long as our eyes are on Him and we are following Him, then at some point along the way, some of the people in the world that have hated us will come to us in their times of despair because they want to find Jesus too. This can lead them to choose to become His disciples too.

Jesus will lead anyone that comes to Him, no matter how dark may be the place they are coming from, so as long as they are following Him. They can follow us for a time, until they can see Him with their own eyes of faith. Isn't that what being a disciple is about? We can only lead others to Jesus if we are indeed following Him.

PRAYER

When did you decide to follow Jesus?

When in your life, if ever, do you know that you took your eyes off Jesus and followed a different path? If you did, what caused you to return?

When in your journey following Jesus have you felt the world hated you? How did you deal with that?

Lord Jesus, help us remember that you followed your Father's perfect will, and that when we follow you, we are following the way to the Father. Holy Spirit, encourage us on our journey that we may stay focused on Jesus and not be distracted or deceived into following any other person or way that will not satisfy our longing for the Way, the Truth and the fullness of Life that you give us. Bring us home safely to you.

Amen.

Discipline – The Fruit of Self-Control

I find it interesting that the root of the word discipleship is discipline. Discipline is one of those "not-feel good" words, yet discipleship has a more positive connotation – at least there is a sense of journey, or even adventure, especially if I am a disciple of a very wise and powerful leader. As a disciple, by definition, I am following someone or some belief system other than myself or my own, respectively. For this reflection, we will be speaking about following Jesus and Christian beliefs.

Perhaps a good place to consider how discipline might fit into discipleship is to look at our own journeys and honestly ask ourselves "Am I following Jesus?" We are taught in Proverbs not to despise the discipline of the Lord. We are loved as sons and daughters and the Lord disciplines those He loves. I remember when I was a middle school teacher and classroom discipline was the greatest challenge for me, especially with that age group. I learned that my ability as a teacher to discipline was paramount to the class being able to learn and for students to feel comfortable. While an unruly classroom may be fun for a while, students are not comfortable if their teacher cannot establish order. Loose isn't free, it is chaos! Students simply do not feel safe without order.

So from the classroom, I learned that discipline is not about being CONTROLLING, but rather it is about establishing ORDER. So together we created classroom rules to live by. Discipline is about following a way and it felt secure to have a way of how we have agreed to conduct ourselves. The other end of the spectrum is when we become too rigid. That too is CONTROLLING. Freedom is ORDER, being in harmony with one's spirit and God.

For us in our spiritual lives, besides understanding basic Christianity and the creed we believe in, we also each have to work out with the Lord how to conduct ourselves in the day to day specific situations we find ourselves in. We are each unique, and how we choose to live out our unique lives has to do with listening for the Lord's direction when we pray. Often that will require us to exercise self-control when we sense that we are resisting Him.

Jesus tells us that "No servant is greater than the master" (John 13:16). Jesus was disciplined - self-disciplined. He was disciplined to pray and carry out the Father's will, and He kept Jewish traditions and feasts.

I can get real discouraged when I look at myself with respect to self-discipline. Let me share some of my observations of myself. I am always trying to get my house in order: cleaning closets, basements, putting things away, throwing away things that no longer fit or belong. Then there is the aspect of trying to be healthy and lose weight! I have a room (or rather a museum) full of equipment – a stepping machine, a rowing machine, a Nordic ski track, a stationary bicycle, and because that wasn't somehow enough, I then got a treadmill! So my collection of machines that I do not use is now complete! I am always losing the same 20 lbs. – that is what I thought Weight Watchers meant by being a lifetime member!

Then, there is the way that I spend the precious gift of time – I procrastinate – I've been writing this book for 30 years! Or looking at how I speak and spend the precious gift of words! My husband said to me once "if it feels too good to say it, it probably should not be said!" Such wisdom! I still have a long way to go to discipline my tongue.

So with that said, I ask myself "Where does the energy come from to be disciplined?" And Scripture tells us quite simply and truthfully, such discipline comes from God – we can't manufacture it on our own. It is one of the fruits of the Holy Spirit listed in Galatians 5:22: the fruit of self-control. Because God knows that our Self needs to be controlled. Once we realize that, and accept that reality, we can begin to follow Jesus.

When we are exerting self-control, in the Spirit, we are truly free. The great irony is that self-control is experienced as FREEDOM. No one else has to control us! When we feel bound, it is that we are bound to other things that are controlling us, rather than our self, or God. God has empowered our true "self" to take control of itself. Each one of us is responsible for our own self. No one can take our journey for us, but God often provides companions along the way who we admire because they have found a way to bring a holy order to their lives, and they can help us to see ourselves.

Once a person has begun to learn self-control, that person can begin to shepherd others. Only then is leadership anointed, or else it becomes controlling. Did you ever notice that often the most controlling people are those who cannot control themselves! Being controlling is NOT leadership. Having one's self and life in order is perfect leadership—leadership that beckons others to follow.

PRAYER

Where are you in the self-control department?

Are you loose, undisciplined, and feeling as though things are always unraveling and overwhelming?

Or,

Are you very rigid, trying to control too many things or other people, or feeling stifled?

What areas are you pleased with in your life, where you have experienced balance and order in your life?

What areas of your life would you like the Holy Spirit to empower you with self-control?

Pray for the fruit of the Holy Spirit of self-control. It will set you free!

Amen.

9

Growth and Transformation

Living in the Spirit does not mean having a perfect life, the bowl of cherries kind. We would prefer to go from one really powerful and anointed experience of God in our lives to another, but the absence of experiences will happen, and at some point we will need to learn to walk by our faith in God's promises, a faith that goes beyond our feelings and involves a decision to trust Him even when the really positive and exciting experiences are few and far between.

During Holy Week in 1977, I had a profound conversion experience that began during the hearing of the Passion gospel and continued in deep prayer and surrendering of my life to Jesus…yet again. But it was different this time. The Holy Spirit had opened my eyes and my heart to connect with Jesus, and once I did, I couldn't deny that He was real, and alive, and that there is a relationship to be lived with Him. This time of deep prayer and conversion resulted in my receiving the supernatural gift of tongues. I was twenty years old and this happened in the privacy of my college apartment bedroom. I thought life would never be the same again! And it wasn't – my world went from black and white to color, and has never gone back. But I also had mistakenly thought that I would be free from struggles, pain and even my sinful nature after having had such a powerful spiritual experience. We all have to continue to live out our lives as exiles here on planet Earth, and we are certainly not yet in heaven while here. I experienced many trials the following year that I could not have endured without the Holy Spirit in my life. God gave me His Holy Spirit when He did because He knew what lay ahead, and that I would need Him in order to survive the emotional pain that was coming my way.

It is not only Christians that suffer in the world! Human beings living out our sentence here on earth all have a cross to bear in this world, not only Christians! The difference is that Christians learn to bring their cross to Jesus, who has already carried it. And He not only carried it, but He transformed it into new life and for good purpose – His victory over the cross! As we walk the path of our individual and unique spiritual journey, we will continue to be called to bring our pain and struggles and sin to His cross so all things can be transformed and so we can move forward.

Not to move forward is to fall backward. We grow and are transformed by being in the presence of God – we cannot change ourselves. We are healed by bringing our true self to our God, into His light, unafraid of His rejection or judgment, but rather to bask in His healing love, accepting His gift of salvation to free us from our sins and woundedness. It will always be a temptation to avoid coming to Him or into His light, but when we do, we are healed and set free.

We must expect some spiritual warfare. This is because when we make a fundamental choice to be with our God, we become the devil's enemy. The evil one does not just sit back and watch and let us grow. He knows our weaknesses and he will always be poking at them. I recall many years ago hearing a Christian comedian named Mike Warnke – it doesn't seem possible that there could be such a thing as a Christian comedian but this guy was quite funny, and he knew the spiritual battle first hand. His journey before finding Jesus was very dark, and he actually was in a satanic cult - he almost died of drug addiction and finding Jesus changed his entire life. One of my favorites of his quotes when dealing with temptation is "If you keep on doing all the do's you don't have time to do the don'ts!"

Spiritual growth is best measured by the fruits of the Holy Spirit not by the gifts of the Holy Spirit. The fruits of the Spirit are listed in Galatians 5: Love, Joy, Peace, Patience, Kindness, Goodness, Faithfulness, Gentleness, and Self-Control. The way to understand the difference between fruits and gifts of the Spirit is that gifts are given to us freely to empower us so that God can work in and through us. The fruits of the Spirit are characteristics of God's nature – and as we grow our nature should start to look more and more like God's nature. We should be able to ask the question "Am I becoming more Christ-like?" For example, if I am in a certain provoking situation, do I still react with uncontrollable anger, or do I sense an ability to choose to have more self-control?

It is good to reflect on and remember what has lifted us up in the past, and allowed us to make more room for God in our lives. For me Praise & Worship, hearing anointed teachings, entering into prayer, reading Scripture and meditating on the Word of God as if God is speaking it directly to me today, into the current circumstances I find myself in, are what helps me break through spiritual down times. Being in small group fellowship and large group community is also powerful in that the prayers of others surround me and strengthen my faith. I don't do all of these things every day, but balance is key, and I need to find a way to integrate these components into my journey.

A friend of mine had a great image for how we continue to grow. She shared the image of a grocery cart, asking the question, "What do you put in your spiritual grocery cart?" Do you fill it with harmful items such as counterfeit spirituality (e.g. fortune telling vs. prophecy,

New Age – you are each gods vs. you are each God's, Reiki, which is not the same thing as charismatic healing prayer). Or do you put junk food in your cart such as watching excessive amounts of TV? We need to carefully choose what we select to live on, to feed ourselves on.

Another one of my favorite quotes is the Native American Cherokee Story – Two Wolves:

> "One evening an old Cherokee told his grandson about a battle that goes on inside people. He said, 'My son, the battle is between two wolves inside us all. One is Evil – It is anger, envy, jealousy, sorrow, regret, greed, arrogance, self-pity, guilt, resentment, inferiority, lies, false pride, superiority, and ego. The other is Good – It is joy, peace, love, hope, serenity, humility, kindness, benevolence, empathy, generosity, truth, compassion and faith.'
>
> The grandson thought about it for a minute and then asked his grandfather: "Which wolf wins?"
>
> The old Cherokee simply replied, 'The one you feed.'"

PRAYER

Baptist preacher E. V. Hill said in a sermon:

"I'm not what I should be, but thanks be to God, I'm not what I used to be!"

Take a moment to reflect on your spiritual life. Ask the Holy Spirit to bring certain aspects to mind, the ones that God wants to show you at this moment.

Do you see progress? Have you grown? Do you see the fruits of the Holy Spirit getting stronger in your life? As long as we are here on earth we will have to contend with temptation and our own sinful nature, but do you sense you are growing in your ability to recognize what it is that leads you away from God?

Take a moment to give thanks for the growth you see in your life.

Take a moment to recommit yourself to choosing to yield to the Holy Spirit – your "yes" to God.

Take a moment to ask the Holy Spirit to lead you in this specific moment to make a choice that leads you closer to God in a situation you find yourself in now.

Amen.

10

Jesus is the Great I AM, and I am Not!

In Genesis, when Moses asked "the voice" coming from the burning bush "Who should I say sent me?", Yahweh God answered him "Tell Pharaoh that I AM sends you." This name was given to Moses by God Himself after he was also given the command to go to Pharaoh to insist that the emperor "Let my people go."

I AM...two simple words...but they convey the eternal and the almighty. God declares He is not just historic, in the past, nor is He only yet to come, in the future, but He is now, in the present moment. I AM. And the unspoken truth conveyed in these words are, I AM, and will always be. Our relationship with God can only happen in the present moment, the great I AM embracing me in the present moment, just as "I am."

It is hard to grasp that the infinite God desires a personal and intimate relationship with the finite creatures He created, me and you. In fact, it is beyond human comprehension. When God reveals Himself to us seeking to draw closer to us, this personal intimacy is so powerful and yet so tender, all at the same time. God also shows us that He is all-knowing, in big and in little ways. Sometimes the little ways are even more powerful because they show us how aware God is of the details of our life, of who we are. He knows us perfectly. He can show us His hand in our life as part of helping us with a minute detail we are struggling with, and we somehow know that He is with us. He shows us that He is aware of what we like and what we don't like, our heart's desires, and our tears. He reveals that He is familiar with all of the little things as well as the big things that throw us into our faith crises. God is so tender and loving and personal that we can misunderstand and begin to believe, knowingly or unknowingly, that the relationship we have with Him is somehow between two equals. The problem with this is we inevitably create a false God, one who is finite, like ourselves, and we lose sight of who He is, and our dependency on Him.

The Father introduced Jesus, and confirmed His identity at His baptism when He says "This is my Beloved Son in whom I am well pleased. Listen to Him". So Jesus was not speaking from delusion or wishful thinking when He spoke about His oneness with the Father. And in His teachings to the crowds He continued to echo the same name...I AM. Not only did He call Himself the Son of Man, which in Jewish understanding was blasphemous because it implied equality with God, but he chose the words "I AM" to describe His identity. Provocatively, in the gospels (John 8:58) Jesus says "Before Abraham was I AM." Then throughout the gospels Jesus reveals His identity through several "I AM" statements. "I AM the bread of life... he who believes in Me will never go hungry." "I AM the light of the world." "I AM the living water –He who drinks of this water will never thirst again." "I AM the Good Shepherd." "I AM the doorway for the sheep..." "I AM the Way, the Truth and the Life."

Jesus clearly was a threat to the Pharisees - He was in their way - but they could not put Him to death for being competition, or for performing signs and wonders to confirm the Word that He spoke. Because Jesus was clear that He and the Father were one, he could be accused of blasphemy, which was punishable by death. This got me thinking that whenever I start to think that I can save the world, or other people, or even myself (which of course proves to be impossible each and every time), there is an underlying blasphemy in my belief system about myself!

Jesus is the great I AM, and I am not!

This is good news for my life. It means that I have a Savior who knows that I cannot save myself or my family or my friends or the world. I can only turn to Him and admit my need for Him. That is when the saving power of the great I AM can be released to work in and through me. Jesus is always working to save the world through those of us that know He is the Savior of the world. The gift and power of the Holy Spirit living within us is the saving grace for the life of the world.

In Corinthians 5 the apostle Paul says "By grace I am what I am…" - I cite this not only as a play on words for this reflection on "I AM" but to confirm that it is grace at work through us that builds the kingdom of God in our midst, here on earth as it is in heaven. The minute we think it is a result of our own goodness or strength we enter into the realm of blasphemous thinking. There is a world of difference between me being God, and God working through me.

Another point to consider is that we often get caught in the pendulum that swings between two extremes: It is all up to me or it is all up to God. And as the saying goes…trust that it is all up to God, but live as if it is all up to you! When it is all up to me, then the burden is upon me to figure out God's plan for my life and make it happen. I have to figure out God's plan for others and make that happen too! I have to, I have to, I have to save the world! And the worst part of this mindset is that on a good day, I even think I can!

Jesus is the great I AM, and I am not!

The other extreme is equally paralyzing – the philosophy that it is all up to God, and that I don't have to do anything – God will make everything happen - just let go and do nothing, get comfortable, stay comfortable. Don't care too much about anyone or anything because it will just become another hassle and responsibility in my life. Don't get involved because caring will become a noose around my neck.

None of us is a Savior – we are created by God for a purpose and it is His Holy Spirit in us that will guide us and empower us. We cannot even control our own lives, we can only seek to be open to what God wants to do through us. Jesus said "Greater things shall you do than I did" and Paul says we continue the ministry of Jesus – we are His hands and His feet now. But!!!! He is the great I AM, and I am not! I have a small part to play - a part that I was created for, gifted for, and will gently be called forth into as I am moved by the Spirit.

Jesus says "Come to me all you who are burdened and heavy laden and I will give you rest. Take My yoke upon you, and learn of Me; for I am meek and lowly in heart: and you shall find rest for your souls. For My yoke is easy and My burden is light." (Matthew 11:28-30). There is a difference between a noose around our neck and a yoke upon our shoulders that has been perfectly fitted for our gifts and desires, and gently placed there by Jesus, according to His will for me. Many of us carry burdens and yokes that were never intended for us, and then do not get the opportunity to carry that yoke that was meant for us to carry, the one that would have brought us joy and fulfillment.

Jesus is the great I AM, and I am not! What a great comfort to realize this! Our role is to allow Jesus to work through us, His way; not to try to tell Him how to save the world based on my limited understanding, selfish perspective, or finite wisdom.

Jesus is the great I AM, and I am not!

Let us breathe a sigh of relief!

PRAYER

Where do you feel burdened? Heavy laden?

What yokes are you carrying? Is it an easy yoke – does it fit you?

Think of a burden that you carry that is light…one that you know you are meant to carry.

What will you do with the other burden that may not have your name on it?

The Serenity Prayer is a good one to consider as to what is mine to do versus what only God can do:

"God grant me the serenity to accept the things I cannot change,

Courage to change the things I can, and

Wisdom to know the difference."

Holy Spirit, give me discernment to know what burdens I should let go of, and to know those which are my responsibility.

Set me free from the extra burdens that I have accepted that are not from You, the ones that break my back rather than comfortably rest on my shoulders.

Lord Jesus, I place all my burdens at your feet, every one that I carry.

Let me go forward lighter, accepting only the yoke you choose to place on my shoulders. The one that is easy and light for the way you designed my shoulders to handle.

I pray as always in the name of Jesus, My Lord,

Amen.

PART III.

THE "DIS-EASE" OF SIN

The Ten Commandments – God's Gift of a Moral Compass

This reflection is based on the premise that God gave Moses the Ten Commandments out of His love for His people, and also because He knows what we are made of; namely, we have a propensity towards sin. With these commandments, God provides a moral compass to the people He loves and wants to protect. The commandments are a road map for how to journey safely in this world.

When considering the commandments in the spirit of God's love for us, rather than as a list of do's and don'ts that keep us from having a joyful life, we can see what sin looks like from God's perspective, and we can learn where the boundary lies between living within the protection of God's love and plan for our lives, versus living outside of that boundary. Living our lives outside that boundary is where we become victims of Satan's world, subject to the consequences of living outside of the protection God has ordained for us.

Especially in our generation, the word "commandment" does not seem to be very relevant, nor does it sound appealing. Yet, the great gift Yahweh gave to Moses for his precious people, the Israelites, were the Ten Commandments written on tablets of stone with fire from God's own finger. Reflecting on this fact, and on the fact that God's motive for providing the commandments was His great love for us, and His knowing that we "know not what we do," let's consider these commandments as positive wisdom for our lives.

The benefit of looking at the commandments in a positive light - as "Thou Shalts" rather than as "Thou Shalt Nots" – is that it helps us see that we have a lot of room to improve, or grow. Most of us believe that we rarely if ever break any of the Ten Commandments. It is easy to dismiss their relevance to our choices and actions. We can lull ourselves into a false sense of security thinking "oh, I am innocent by those standards!" So with this focus, let us take a new look at the Ten Commandments and try to understand more deeply the guidance and wisdom that God was providing to us.

I am the Lord thy God...You shall have no other gods but Me.

Do you hear the cry in God's heart through these words? God is not debating His position; rather He is clearly telling us who He is, and telling us that we will be outside of our relationship with Him if we seek or have other gods. In my heart I hear this commandment as "I AM enough for you. Allow me to be your God." It is a call to be faithful to Him and to go to Him first with our needs. We may think we do not have any other gods. Well, try evaluating yourself against Mike Warnke's definition of a false god: "... a false god is that which you turn to in your moment of need." Do I turn to the One True God? Or do I turn to television, fortune tellers, pornography, other religions, new age practices, drugs, alcohol, etc. Wow...now I find myself wondering if perhaps there is an entire legion of false gods in my spiritual life!

Who or what do I turn to in my moment of need?

You shall not make for yourself an idol in the form of anything.

This commandment speaks about carving an image or worshiping an image. Many Protestants believe Catholics violate this commandment when they have images of saints carved in statues, but let's consider an even deeper meaning. When we make something, we become the creator. It is as if we believe we can define, create, and contain our God in the image we make Him to be. Our created image is always going to be lacking, because we are the created, not the Creator. God alone is the Creator, and the One True God. We limit God when we worship a god of our own making, when we think we have God all figured out and can contain him in a nice neat little box, or on a stand, or on a necklace, or make Him "just like me", we will always be surprised when we realize that we are way too finite and imperfect to ever be able to grasp the infinite omnipotent loving God that we are called to know and worship as Father, Son and Holy Spirit.

The worst false god is the one of our own making.

You shall not misuse the name of the Lord your God. Other translations say *"Thou shall not take the name of the Lord thy God in vain."*

This commandment is packed with God's revelation of Himself to us. The most common understanding of this commandment is that we are not to use the name of God when uttering a profanity. This is certainly true at face value, but there is another lesson to be learned in this command.

God's name is *sacred.* In the Old Testament, after Moses saw the burning bush, he asks the voice coming from the bush "What is your name?" Sharing one's name is a first step in beginning to know someone. God reveals His name as "I Am"…Yahweh is actually a contracted name because God's name was too sacred to write or utter. We cannot put God in a box. He cannot be contained by a name. In the New Testament, we are given the Name of Jesus as the only name by which we are saved. We approach the Father through Jesus, and we pray in Jesus' name.

If God's name is sacred and powerful, then perhaps we also take His name in vain when we do not pray in His name, failing to realize the gift – His name – that we have been given to invoke when we call out to Him. We can also take His name in vain when we fail to realize the power that Jesus has been given by the Father. We are told in Philippians 2:10, "At the name of Jesus, every knee shall bow, and every tongue confess, that Jesus Christ is Lord! "

So when we fail to recognize the Lordship of Jesus and fail to pray in His name, we can take His name in vain by rendering it powerless in our life circumstances. The name of Jesus can never be powerless, but its power can fail to be released in our lives if we fail to recognize who Jesus is and revere His holy name.

Remember the Sabbath day by keeping it holy.

We often think of this commandment as the literal directive by God that we have to go to church every Sunday. I think by now you must sense that I don't like to stop at literal interpretations, but believe there is deep meaning to everything God speaks to us. When I look at myself, and the world around me, our Smartphones are constantly in hand or within reach. I can't tell you how many times my husband says "take your phone with you!" even when I am going to take a shower! Why? So I know that someone tried to reach me. Where have our private moments gone? It is scary really, to think we are so constantly available to anyone that has our number! I have heard multiple speakers say that the God who loves us so much is calling us to reserve at least one seventh of our allotted time in this life to the sacredness of the gift of rest; to spend such time on love and loved ones, on rest, on reflection, on quiet moments of reflection, rather than immersed in the flood of constant communication and input from the world. It is a loving gift of rest that our Father is asking us to receive. When I think of it that way, it is such a breath of fresh air...a pause, one day out of seven...where I can rest and reflect and rejuvenate.

God says to us "Spend one seventh of your life for rest and rejuvenation, because I love you."

Honor your father and your mother.

For me, this commandment is a call to Choose Life, to respect the gift of life...my life...all life....from womb to tomb as they say. This understanding of the commandment makes sense to me, as we aren't all equally fortunate to have had a wonderful father and a mother in our lives. Some people have been very wounded by dysfunctional parents and homes, making this commandment another stab in the heart. But when we hear it as a call to appreciate the gift of our life...that somehow we are here now and have a life to live through the ancestry of our father and mother, then no matter how good or bad we were parented, healing can come when we realize that we all have the same perfect Father in heaven, Our Father, who loves us perfectly. Perhaps honoring parents in such circumstances means forgiving them so that we can move on enjoying the gift of our life.

God is saying "Respect the gift of your life. It is honorable, and holy. And so are you."

You shall not murder.

We tend to think of this commandment as an easy one. Most of us have never taken the physical life of another, so we rest in feeling assured we are not guilty of breaking this commandment. But rather than hearing this as a command not to kill anyone, to me this is again a call to Choose Life. Even deeper than that is the call to build up one another rather than kill one another. There are many ways to kill one another besides taking someone's physical life. As stated in "All I Really Needed to Know I Learned in Kindergarten" by Robert Fulghum, we can kill each other with words and gossip. The author powerfully and insightfully states "Sticks and stones will break our bones but names will break our hearts." Wow...how many times have I broken this commandment?

God is saying "Use your voices to bless, not to destroy, one another."

You shall not commit adultery.

You probably have caught my drift by now…rather than hearing this as I can't cheat on my spouse, the deeper call is to be faithful to commitments we have made, to vows we have spoken, and to our relationships. We are called to value the relationships we have chosen to be responsible for, and to. "Let your yes mean yes, and your no mean no." (Matthew 5:37).

God is saying "Be faithful to your promises; uphold the words you speak."

You shall not steal.

The obvious understanding of this is not to take something that belongs to someone else. Another way to hear this commandment is "Do not take what is not yours." Or in a positive directive, "Give what you do not need to the needy." I heard Father Richard Rohr say in a homily "God alone gives…we exchange." God gives us plenty – remember the leftover baskets of loaves and fishes - but we need to find a way to share that which He has given.

None of us owns any of it. It all belongs to God.

God is saying "Take what you need, and share the rest."

You shall not give false testimony against your neighbor.

This is pretty clear…it is wrong to speak falsely (aka false testimony), and badly (aka against), about another person. To me this relates to the essence of "thou shalt not kill," because our slander and gossip can destroy a person's reputation and life. It is also a call to Speak Truth.

We can even take this one step further in love…if we are called to do unto others as we would want them to do unto us, then we would be very grateful if someone took the time to speak truthfully about something good we have done.

God is saying "Speak the truth."

You shall not covet your neighbor's house, wife or property.

The word covet is powerful…you can feel its pull when you speak it. It is a death grip, really. It keeps us bound in ungratefulness, believing we have been gypped somehow, that we have less than everyone else. I saw a plaque that had the quote "Happiness is wanting what you have, not having what you want." There would be so much more peace and tranquility residing in our soul if we appreciated what we do have, not seeing what we don't have, or looking at what others have, and wanting it instead. God knows us perfectly, and provides for each of us according to His purpose and will for our lives, and according to the true desires that have been planted in our hearts. I find that if I say thank you every day for things that I do have, I feel richly blessed. When I look at what others have, I feel inadequate and resentful.

Coveting is a demon that is so common we can easily forget how destructive it is to our soul.

God is saying "Appreciate what you have, and what you have been given."

PRAYER:

Take a moment to reflect on the commandments.

Ask the Holy Spirit to bring to mind which one He is inviting you to pray about related to your life at this time.

Which commandment are you drawn to?

The 10 Commandments are a great gift to help us identify the sin that makes us sick.

SIN ALWAYS GETS WORSE. That small stone in your shoe somehow turns into the millstone around your neck. We often tolerate the small pebble and then later we find we are surprised that we are in a painful and difficult place, because the pebble has now become a huge stone that we cannot move even if we want to.

Let go of sin as soon as the Holy Spirit reveals it to you.

Thank you Father God for loving us so much that you provide a moral compass for us to live by.

Amen.

The Battle in my Mind – My Personal Sin

Have you heard the saying "If you don't know you are in a battle then you are probably losing it!"? So it is in our Christian walk – we are called to be followers of Jesus Christ and we don't often think of that as involving spiritual warfare; yet we suffer the wounds of battle, don't we? We feel defeated, discouraged, afraid or guilty; and we are often being robbed of our joy and our peace in Christ.

The word "battle" seems incongruous to us as A.D. Christians, using words such as "warfare" and "spiritual battle", or "fighting our enemy," when Jesus taught us to forgive even our enemies. So let us consider this fight in the way Jesus taught us to when He said to the disciples in Matthew:

Matthew 10:16: "See, I am sending you out like sheep into the midst of wolves; so be wise as serpents and innocent as doves."

Clearly Jesus warns us that there are wolves, and there is Satan (whose name means "adversary"), and there is a battle. One of Satan's biggest strategies is to get us to doubt his existence, or to forget that we know of his existence. To this doubt Jesus reminds us:

Luke 10:18: He said to them, "I watched Satan fall from heaven like a flash of lightning. ¹⁹See, I have given you authority to tread on snakes and scorpions, and over all the power of the enemy; and nothing will hurt you. [20]Nevertheless, do not rejoice at this, that the spirits submit to you, but rejoice that your names are written in heaven."

In Romans 7:15 Paul laments: "For that which I am doing, I do not understand; for I am not practicing what I would like to do, but I am doing the very thing I hate."

And in 2 Corinthians 12:7 he says: "A thorn was given me in the flesh, a messenger of Satan to torment me. "

Paul was tempted, we certainly know that Peter and Judas were tempted, and even Jesus was tempted during His desert fast. So too are we. There is a battle.

For this reflection, I am considering the aspect of our battle to be one of defense rather than offense. There are some that God uniquely calls and equips for deliverance ministry – but most of us are called to deal with evil in the way of personal temptation and intercession for those we love when they are tempted.

It is important to remember that there is **not an equal war** between God and Satan. God is supreme, and the devil is a creature, not the Creator. The devil is finite, God is infinite. This is evident in the Scripture from ***Revelations 12:12:*** Rejoice then, you heavens and those who dwell in them! But woe to the earth and the sea, for the devil has come down to you with great wrath, because he knows that his time is short!"

In 1 Peter 5:8-9 we hear: "Discipline yourselves, keep alert. Like a roaring lion your adversary the devil prowls around, looking for someone to devour. Resist him, steadfast in your faith, for you know that your brothers and sisters in all the world are undergoing the same kinds of suffering."

Satan is hungry for our allegiance by using our free will to yield to his deception; and Satan is hungry for our lives.

Just as it is not an equal war between God and Satan, it is also not an equal war between Satan and ourselves. We are human, and the devil and his demons are spiritual beings. We, on our own, are not a match for the father of lies.

"For our struggle is not against enemies of blood and flesh, but against the rulers, against the authorities, against the cosmic powers of this present darkness, against the spiritual forces of evil in the heavenly places." (Ephesians 6:12).

We cannot take Satan on. It is only Jesus' victory on the cross over sin and death that gives us authority over the enemy. Never challenge evil on your own merit, your own worthiness, your own giftedness or your own power. Sin can only be removed by the blood of Jesus, at the cross, and only by the authority of His Name. That is why we conclude our prayers "in the name of Jesus," for there is no other name by which we are to be saved (Acts 4:12).

We need to think this way and I am writing this because I realize that I often don't think this way, and perhaps you don't either. Whatever is in my head I listen to, whatever I see I take in, whatever I hear I listen to. I hardly ever think about the need to protect myself. How can we protect ourselves as Christians? Paul graphically explains our protection in Ephesians 6:11 – 18: "Put on the whole armor of God"

[11]Put on the whole armor of God, so that you may be able to stand against the wiles of the devil. [12]For our struggle is not against enemies of blood and flesh, but against the rulers, against the authorities, against the cosmic powers of this present darkness, against the spiritual forces of evil in the heavenly places. [13]Therefore take up the whole armor of God, so that you may be able to withstand on that evil day, and having done everything, to stand

firm. [14]Stand therefore, and fasten the belt of truth around your waist, and put on the breastplate of righteousness. [15]As shoes for your feet put on whatever will make you ready to proclaim the gospel of peace. [16]With all of these, take the shield of faith, with which you will be able to quench all the flaming arrows of the evil one. [17]Take the helmet of salvation, and the sword of the Spirit, which is the word of God.

[18]Pray in the Spirit at all times in every prayer and supplication. To that end keep alert and always persevere in supplication for all the saints.

Quite the outfit! Ironically this is the same armor that young David wore when he fought the giant, Goliath. David didn't want to be encumbered with the traditional metal armor worn by the Israelites, but rather he wanted to stand only on his faith in the authority and strength of God, the same way he fought the lion and the bear when his sheep were being attacked.

What is my personal sin? How do I know what is my sin – not the sin of the world, but my individual contribution to the sin in the world?

When (if) we received the Holy Spirit, we received the presence of Jesus living within us 24/7. In Gospel John 16:8, Jesus told the disciples that one role of the Holy Spirit working in a believer's life is to convict us of our sin. God's promise through the gift of the Spirit is that we will be made aware, in the depths of our hearts, of when we are stumbling into dangerous spiritual ground. It is a gift that we no longer have to rely on a high priest or others to tell us what is sin; nor do we have to depend upon our own logic to discover that we are in sin. The Lord has promised to gently whisper it in our hearts, coming from His omnipotence. His law is now written on our hearts rather than on tablets of stone.

If we are honest, we will admit that we aren't delighted about this gift. Why not? I think we don't really understand how bad sin is, and the damage it does to us, so we are not able to grasp how much we need God's protection as we walk through our life journey. Also, the human reaction to the gift of the Holy Spirit to "convict us of our sin" is negative because it hurts our pride. We don't always want to know our sin – we would rather tolerate it and we are deceived into thinking that we can manage it on our own, or that it is hidden, and doesn't show.

The next chapter deals with how our personal sin not only devours us, but contributes to the corporate sin of the world – another reason we need to deal with our sin and God wants to reveal it to us. We all want to change the world but grimace at the thought of starting with "me." As our Counselor, the Holy Spirit's role to convict us of sin is to free us of our pain and our deceptions. The hard part is that it requires our humility to recognize our sin and bring it to the cross in true repentance - to make the choice to get rid of it. It requires our humility to repent and be set free. It also takes trust to leave our sin there, and move on trusting in the Lord's forgiveness through the blood of Jesus.

We really can't pretend or deny that we feel "pings from our conscience" when God tries to get us to pause and consider our movement and motivation. This is an amazing testimony to the real and living presence of the Holy Spirit within us – a great gift – that we can KNOW when we sin! We "feel" it! This is meant to be good news, but of course, because of our human nature, and fear, it is something that we want to resist, or worse, resent and rebel against. We suffer from the deception that "our" sin is ok, or "just a little sin is ok, as long as I keep it in check." As if we have power over it on our own! Sin begins like a small stone in our shoe – it aggravates us a little, but because we can still walk, and even start to develop a callous on our foot to no longer feel it as much, we think "no problem, I can live with this." But when we allow sin to grow in us, to take root, it eventually becomes the millstone around our neck. And we wonder how things got so bad. Sin ALWAYS gets worse! In James 1:12-16 we read about the progression of desire to sin. We don't realize how deadly sin is. The wages of sin is death (Romans 6:23). Not sometimes, but always.

This is an interesting dilemma that we suffer given our human nature. God promises to reveal our sin to us personally. Yet He continues to give us a free choice to decide what we will do with that revelation. Sometimes we humans fear that God will completely take us over, and that we will lose our freedom when we surrender our lives to Him. In fact, it is quite the opposite! We will never lose our freedom when we surrender to Him, on two accounts. One is that He will allow us to choose our sin instead of repenting of it. The other aspect is that once we do repent of the identified sin, we will experience true freedom, more than we have ever known! Satan deceives us into fearing this loss of our freedom. I have been on this spiritual journey long enough to now find myself wishing that God would take my freedom away from me, and cause me to choose rightly, according to His will for my life. But our free will is a gift that He will never take away from us.

The Holy Spirit does not come upon us and bombard us with all that is "wrong with us." And, the conviction of the Holy Spirit does not feel like judgment or condemnation. It is oddly liberating! Like getting a proper diagnosis from a doctor when you know something isn't right. It brings peace to get a right diagnosis and to understand what is causing the sickness within. This is true for our spiritual health as well.

It is good to pray and listen, and ask the Holy Spirit to come and show one area of our life that is out of order. This is one of those for sure answered prayers...ask and you shall receive! Seek and you shall find! Knock and it shall be opened unto you!

We are not alone. In 1 John, verses 5-10, we hear that all are sinners – if we think we are not then we are calling God a liar. Jesus died for sinners. The really simple message and truth is: I am a sinner and I needed Jesus to die for me to save my eternal life:

> *"This is the message we have heard from him and proclaim to you, that God is light and in him there is no darkness at all. If we say that we have fellowship with him while we are walking in darkness, we lie and do not do what is true; but if we walk in the light as he himself is in the light, we have fellowship with one another, and the blood of Jesus his Son cleanses us from all sin. If we say that we have no sin, we deceive ourselves, and the truth is not in us. If we confess our sins, he who is faithful and just will forgive us our sins and cleanse us from all unrighteousness. If we say that we have not sinned, we make him a liar, and his word is not in us. "*

When we stop trying to deny or justify our sin, then we begin to win the battle in our mind. But what do we do with our sin? The answer again is simple – I am to "bring it to the cross" where Jesus has already paid the price for it and conquered it for me. Of course, we will spend our life on earth learning to do that sooner than later. Bringing our sin to the cross means we get to exchange our helplessness and inability to conquer it with Jesus' victory over it already. We get to hear the words "Forgive them Father, for they know not what they do." We can exchange our filthy rags for new and clean garments! Jesus died once and for all, for all sin. Let us take our sin to the cross, and allow the power of the cross to work for us.

We often talk about "carrying our cross" in this world to share in the suffering of Christ. But this bringing of our sin to the cross is not the same thing as carrying our cross. Jesus has already not only carried this cross, but has also died upon it. We come to the cross to bow before this great gift of our salvation, and to receive it. Jesus gave us this gift of salvation by humbling Himself to death on a cross, is it any wonder that we have to humble ourselves to receive the gift?

The cross provides the way "Up and Out" of the battle. Hence we say "embrace the cross" – it is the means to freedom. Get yourself to the cross and let the blood of Jesus wash over your sin. It is the only cure.

The Holy Spirit also guides us into avoiding sin if we can listen for that prompting to go a different way. In Hebrews 4:15-16 we are told that Jesus was tempted in every way we were, yet did not sin. We are also told in the gospels that Jesus would arise early each day and go to a quiet place to pray to His Father. When is the last time you started your day as Jesus did – asking the Father what you can do today to fulfill His will? Father, what is Your Will for me today? If you are like me, you start the day asking God to do all kinds of things on your behalf or on the behalf of others. Something like "don't let this happen, please let this happen" etc., etc. We direct the Father rather than receiving direction from Him! What if we were to simply show up reporting for duty in the kingdom praying "let Your will be done in and through me today"?

Sometimes the Holy Spirit reveals sin to us through our feelings of hurt or woundedness. Because sin hurts and destroys, often our sin is embedded in our hurt feelings. Often when we ask ourselves the question "Where do I hurt" we will find that the answer is the same as it is to the question "What sin do I allow to remain at work in me?" God's motive is always pure, and pure love for us. He sent His only Son Jesus to die to take our sin away, and He sends us His Holy Spirit to dwell within the temple of our being so we will no longer be ensnared in our sin.

There is also a side benefit to acknowledging our sin and that is, we become less judgmental of others. When we see ourselves as redeemed and forgiven sinners, we can begin to withhold our judgment of others. We all suffer from different vulnerabilities to temptation, we have different weaknesses. But we are all in this together; no matter how few or how many our sins may be numbered, none of us escapes at least having one. And as soon as we think we have no sin, well, unfortunately, that is the sin of pride and arrogance at work!

I heard a preacher on the radio say , "The devil is supposed to be under your feet! If Satan is whispering in your ear then you have allowed him to be in the wrong place in your life." Either you are stooping too low to listen to him, or you have allowed him to deceive you and you have raised him up too high, too close to your ear.

Let us lay aside every weight and the sin that clings to us! (Hebrews 12:1-13)

PRAYER

Where is evil blocking you? As you walk the Way of Jesus, where do you come to a dead stop, as if physically blocked, to continue walking forward? Ask the Holy Spirit to show you an area of sin in your life.

Lord Jesus, You are the Way, please remove this block from my pathway, I pray.

What are the lies or deceptions that have a hold over you? What fears feed your mind? What thoughts fill your mind? What do you believe is true, and how do those beliefs measure against the Word of God? What do you choose for entertainment? How do you fill your free time?

Lord Jesus, You are the Truth, please speak your Truth to this deception, I pray.

Where do you feel wounded and hurt? There is a connection between woundedness and sin. Our sin causes wounds to ourselves and others. We always need to repent of our sin – meaning, we need to name sin as sin and give it to Jesus. We also need to believe it truly is deadly. We need to break our agreement with sin, even if our feelings are not yet there.

Sometimes our hurts come from sins committed by others against us. Those hurts require us to forgive anyone who has hurt us. Our forgiving does not imply it was OK for them to hurt us, rather, it releases us from their continued power over us to keep repeating the offense against us.

Lord Jesus, You forgave us from the cross. Please show me who I most need to forgive and give me the grace to even try to make this choice, I pray.

What kind of darkness oppresses you? Is it guilt? Fear? Deliberate sin? Addiction to drugs, materialism, illicit sexuality, the occult, witchcraft, psychics, unforgiveness, murder, stealing, bitterness, pride, hatred, jealousy?

And it is no wonder! Even Satan disguises himself as an angel of light. So it is not strange if his ministers also disguise themselves as ministers of righteousness. Their end will match their deeds. 2 Corinthians 11:14-15

Lord Jesus, You are the Light, please bring your Light into this darkness, I pray.

I pray in the Name of Jesus of Nazareth, who is seated at the right hand of the Father and has authority over all evil, claiming the power of His cross and resurrection over my life.

Bring your sin to the cross – picture yourself walking up to the cross, to Jesus. Hear Jesus tell you He is dying to set you free from that sin and from its power over you.

Accept Jesus' death on the cross for this particular sin in your life.

Ask the Holy Spirit to empower you – to fill the weak and empty part of you where this sin was rooted.

Of course, the more deeply rooted this sin is, the longer you have been in agreement with it, the more prayer this may take. Sometimes healing is instantaneous, sometimes a process. Whenever you are tempted in this area again, claim your choice to repent of it and try to stand on the power of the Holy Spirit within you rather than on the power of the temptation.

Lord Jesus, I come before you honestly, willing to be molded and changed by you – willing to be set free. May I truly be changed into your image of me. May I learn to trust in your love more than in the deceptive luring power of temptation to sin. I ask this through Jesus Christ my Lord.

Amen.

3

The Battle in the World - Corporate Evil

We all sense it - even those that do not believe in God - there is something wrong with the world. After years of learning how to put a man on the moon, soaring the galaxy getting magnificent pictures of stars and planets and specimens of celestial bodies, and many advances in medicine, we still haven't learned how to stop wars, murders, world hunger, and abuse, to name a few. In essence, we have to admit we have not been able to remove evil from the world with all our efforts and skill. That evil has a name, sin. We have not been able to remove sin from the world. That should come as no surprise, in that each of us as individuals is not able to remove evil from our own hearts.

In the last chapter I address personal sin. In this chapter the reflection is on the corporate evil in the world. I think it is easier for us to see because it does not take nearly the humility that recognizing our own personal sin requires. It is much easier to step back, look at the world, and pass judgments...e.g. "this group of people is violent," or "this denomination is wrong," or "this political party is evil"...when it comes to our own selves and our own personal sin, we are humbled when we see that the evil we despise in the world corporately lurks in our own heart as well. I wonder if God allows this world to continue in spite of the atrocities that humankind continue to defend, so that perhaps we can see what sin really is, as God sees it, and how damaging it is. What if our only hope to ever come to personal repentance is to see our own contribution to corporate evil? Because of Jesus' victory on the cross, the devil must operate under your feet if you have accepted His gift of salvation for you personally.

There is another important reality... evil can also work through me and adversely affect the world. We do not want to hear of the possibility that the evil that I tolerate within myself actually contributes to and becomes part of the world's evil. After all, the world's evil is the sum of the evil in each one of us. When we agree with Satan, we help establish his kingdom here on earth. When we choose Jesus, we help establish God's kingdom here on earth. We all want to abolish evil in the world, but it is a different commitment to the abolishment of evil when it comes to honestly looking within and choosing to renounce the evil that is in my own personal soul.

When I repent and bring my sin to the cross (which is the only way to get rid of it), then I am also in that very moment freeing the world of some of the weight of evil that is upon it; evil that seeps into the world via my own contribution to it. Thus, the hope that I can help change the world for good is realized each time I say a personal yes to God!

So I got to thinking...it helps to realize that we have only one enemy, Satan – Lucifer, the angel of light and the father of lies. People are in his grip. We need to pray for them to be set free. They are not the enemy; rather, they are victims that have been caught and our love and prayers are needed to help release them. You have a right to choose to build God's kingdom and to be safe while doing so.

Jesus again is our role model. He started each day with intimate quiet time in relationship with His Father. Then He got up and started walking into the day, setting out to do good – to accomplish His Father's will and the task at hand of building the kingdom. He is the

Way, the Truth and the Light – He confronted evil when it was in His path and commanded it to move out of His way. Whether He encountered sickness, possession by evil spirits, storms at sea, sinful choices, the death of His friend, or even His own temptation, Jesus commanded the evil to move aside and give way to the kingdom of God. Evil had to move, or leave. When people were lost, He showed them the Way. When people were believing lies & deception, He spoke the Truth, and where there was darkness He brought His Light.

We are called to do the same.

PRAYER

Spend some time reflecting on the world – what is the evil you see in the world that is very apparent to you and really grieves you? Something you wish you could change…something worth fighting for with your own time and voice.

Do you see a connection between this sin in the world and your own area of weakness? Or,

Is this sin in the world an area of strength for you, a sin that you are not tempted by?

Spend some time and pray for the world related to this evil that you see…if the Holy Spirit is bringing this to your mind, or putting it on your heart, then you are called to intercede.

Pray that individuals will cooperate with grace and become aware of this evil, not only in the world, but perhaps in yourself as well.

Amen.

Consequences of Sin – the Real Penance

We follow our hearts desires and often find ourselves in a very wrong place.

God always calls us to repentance but for some reason we need to play out our wrong choice. I wonder why we do this…to prove we are *right*; or to somehow prove that God's ways are *wrong*, or changeable…at least changeable to the extent that I can still be happy enough with them, even if less than ideal? All I know is this…God's laws cannot be changed…Jesus says in (Matthew 24:35, Mark 13:31) "Heaven and earth will pass away but my Words will never pass away." None of us humans wrote them, and try as we may to throw down the tablets they are written on, they come back to us, because they are written by Truth.

God's laws are not there to control or punish us, but oddly, to protect us from danger. We just don't get that.

When we enter into true repentance, and realize our diversion from God's path, we are welcomed back with open arms. Truly God rejoices and we are safe in His arms. However, the consequences of where our choices have led us remain. We cannot undo our own history. At least for the remainder of our life on planet earth, the consequences will be a reminder to us that we can't get the moment back where we had a choice to make and deliberately made it our own way, against God's plan of peace and joy for our lives. It is not a punishment, but I do believe it is our penance.

Before we make a wrong turn, the Holy Spirit often shows us in advance by giving us a sense of disharmony – either a feeling within that this is wrong, or by sending others to us that we know love and care about us, with no ulterior motive but to speak to us that they are not at peace with what we are doing or about to do. The pattern of human nature is that we choose to continue down that wrong path that for some reason we are just "hell-bent" on pursuing.

Can you think of a time where you altered your plans to do things God's way? I am sad to say I don't recall such a time. At this stage of my life I see clearly in hindsight how many wrong choices I made, against the strong warning given to me by beautiful people in my life that were trying to love me and guide me.

Don't get me wrong, it is not hopeless. I know God has a perfect plan to heal all of us...and my hope is that when we are free from this world and living with God in the next, that we will be free not only of our sinful nature, but also from the consequences that we had to live with during our lifetime. And even while we are living out our time on planet earth, He will always help us make the best choices for where we find ourselves today.

If only we would listen to His voice right away we could minimize the amount of difficult consequences we rack up going forward!

When considering consequences of sin, it is important to remember forgiveness of our sin. We live with consequences but we are cleansed and freed from our sin when we accept God's forgiveness. I was remembering when the Israelites were journeying in the desert on their way to the Promised Land, after they were miraculously led out of Egypt by the Lord. God provided manna every morning for them to eat. It is interesting that God commanded them to take and eat what they needed to feed their families, but not to hoard or store the manna overnight. God wanted them to trust that He would again provide for them the next day. Some disobeyed this command and stored manna, only to find it was full of maggots and rotten the next day. Somehow I sensed the Lord showing me the importance of letting go of my sin after He has forgiven it. Hanging onto it keeps it's rotten and decaying presence upon me. When we truly repent of our sin, and grieve it, and ask for the grace to "avoid the near occasion" of that sin, we can rejoice that God has provided the way through the blood of Jesus to make us clean, even as we endure, with His help, the circumstances our sin choices created.

PRAYER

What consequences of sin in your life are especially difficult for you?

Bring them to the Lord, asking Him to help you make the best decisions for your life given the circumstances that cannot be changed.

Praise the Lord for the consequences that can be changed.

The Serenity Prayer comes to mind:

Lord, grant me the serenity to

Accept the things I cannot change,

Courage to change the things I can, and

Wisdom to know the difference.

Ask the Lord to show you ...

Pray for the grace to not keep looking back once you have been forgiven.

Is there a situation that you find you keep coming back to? Give it to the Lord again and ask Him to show you why you are still stuck reliving it.

If you fear that the Lord has not or cannot forgive you, talk to Him about that. Is there still an aspect of that situation's sin that you are "in agreement with", meaning, you have not really turned away from but still try to justify?

Repent and believe the Good News.

If the Lord has forgiven you, then you need to forgive yourself.

Amen.

5

The Peak of "My" Ministry

First of all, if I am speaking about "My" ministry, I am already off-base. None of us owns a ministry, and "if the Lord does not build, they labor in vain who build." (Psalms 127:1) Our work for the Lord is all the Lord's ministry - we are the hands and feet and voices that He uses to serve the people He loves.

I can't help but reflect on my life in Christ, and wonder if I was pleasing to Him at each past stage, or even more importantly, if I am pleasing to Him now. I don't want to waste my life another minute on what is not pleasing to God. There is so little time to a lifespan!

What matters in the end is as the song "When Its All Been Said and Done" by Jim Cowan states "did I do my best to live for Truth, did I live my life for Him?"

I am in transition, having moved out of the state of Connecticut for the first time in 63 years. My parents are still in the house I grew up in from when I was 9 months old until 24 years when I finally moved out (or moved on!) It is a unique blessing to be able to revisit my childhood bedroom at 63 years old, complete with hand scrawls on some of the not so conspicuous walls! Change is hard for me. Moving on happens in small steps of surrender, fighting all the way. I'm not proud of this, just sayin'....

There was a time that I look back on, in my 20s, 30s and 40s, where I was very active in teaching and preaching ministry. I was a leader in just about any community I joined, and was recognized for helping people find their faith in God. That is wonderful, right? It is wonderful until it comes to a screeching halt. Then I can't help but wonder what I have done wrong, because that is how I am wired. Like Moses in Exodus, did I strike the rock instead of speak to it? Which really means, did I do things My Way, or the Old Familiar Way, instead of following Jesus His Way?

I was praying in my vacuum, asking God if I was falling prey to a spirit of sloth, or laziness, or disobedience, or deafness to His call; or to my pride, which enjoyed the positive affirmation of others as to the eloquence or inspiration of my teachings. I travel a lot now that we are retired, and I bring my crucifix with me. I had the crucifix laying on the nightstand next to my bed, and it was positioned in such a way that I could see the face of Jesus looking at me. In my spirit I heard Him say

"This is what the peak of *My* ministry looks like".

The cross. Complete abandonment "My God My God, Why have You Forsaken Me?" I can almost hear Jesus saying from the cross "will it last? The teachings, the healings, the prayers…will they remember what I did and taught them?"

I know that the ministry of the Cross ALSO INCLUDES Resurrection…that the peak of Jesus's ministry is the cross and resurrection. But resurrection can only follow the cross. Jesus says "Very truly I tell you, unless a grain of wheat falls to the ground and dies, it remains only a single seed. But if it dies, it produces many seeds." (John 12:24)

I trust that in my desire to serve Him, He will find a way to use me in my current life circumstances, even if I am allowed to live to be

120 years old. My life will always have as its primary purpose to love and serve Him. So we must trust that He allows and orchestrates our lives to fulfill what He sees to be the way to build His kingdom here on earth. He is so perfect, that even when He is building His kingdom here on earth, He is also building His kingdom in me. Sometimes we need to be stripped of those things we think are our gifts. Sometimes we do the right things for the wrong reasons, or vice versa. So we must offer ourselves to Him for His purposes, His Way.

After all, it is His Ministry, not Mine.

PRAYER

Lord, I know it is Your will that I serve You. But I don't always know what that should look like, or what gifts you are empowering me with at this moment, for such a time as this.

I also cannot see or imagine the change that is needed for my own good so that I may continue to grow and grow closer to You.

I ask that in the Name of Jesus, any reliance that I have on anything other than You be broken; specifically dependence on:

my own abilities

my own ideas

my need for affirmation

my need for acceptance

my need for recognition

my need to feel confident

my need to feel important or needed

my need to withdraw into complaceny or self-pity.

other....

May my life continue to serve you even when I cannot see what You are doing in my life and in the lives of those around me.

Amen.

6

Surrendering to God –True Freedom

Most of us do not associate the word surrender with freedom, and in fact, it seems like a complete contradiction. In the gospels we hear Jesus call us to lay down our lives (that is, to surrender them), take up our cross and follow Him. He says "whoever loses his life for my sake will find it."…If we are honest, none of these statements sounds very appealing, to say the least. As baptized Christians, we are called to surrender ourselves to our Living God, and we struggle with that. The human heart, on the other hand, has a constant and great yearning to be set free. Jesus says in the gospels "You shall know the truth and the truth shall set you free." There is freedom in Christ! When the Spirit sets us free we are free indeed. So, how do we reconcile the feeling of contradiction when we hear that we need to surrender ourselves to Jesus in order to be free? And, what is the freedom we seek? Freedom *from* what? Freedom *for* what?

Part of the problem is that we do not realize that we were created to serve God – it's in our spiritual DNA so to speak. If we do not serve God, then we WILL serve some other master. Jesus came to us as the Master who says "I no longer call you servants, because a servant does not know his master's business. Instead I have called you friends, for everything that I learned from my Father I have made known to you."

(John 15:15) It is ironic that we think we are hanging onto our "freedom" when we withhold our commitment of our life to serve Jesus. This is a great illusion because in fact we are in bondage to some other master that we may or may not be aware of; we can never escape the reality that we will serve some master.

I've stumbled onto the word master a lot lately...for example there are Yogi masters and Reiki masters, sadly even within our Christian churches. Jesus says you cannot serve two masters for you will love the one and hate the other.

When we give our life to Jesus, we serve a master that loves us, one whose only motive is to protect us and lead us safely home to our Father in heaven. We are not safe without aligning ourselves to Jesus. He is the only way to the Father. We are truly free when we choose to give our allegiance to Him.

If we do not, we are in a bondage to a different master – perhaps to our own madness and obsession for things, money, prestige, addictions to substances or even to people – the things that make us feel driven, that take away our peace. I love the bumper sticker that says:

"No Jesus, No Peace. Know Jesus, Know Peace."

It is our illusion of being free without Him that is the greatest bondage of all. Jesus is the only Master that truly sets us free.

We are all victims of this deception. It is the root of the lie the serpent told Adam and Eve in the Garden of Eden. They succumbed to the temptation to doubt God's word to them. God told them they were beautiful, and they were. God told them they were loved, and they were. God told them they were called to be in relationship with each other and they were. God told them they were called to be in relationship with Him, even though He was the Creator and they were the created, and they were, and took walks in the Garden with Him. He provided many trees for them to eat from, but then warned them not to eat of the one tree that would introduce death, tears, pain and exile from the Garden, but they did, because they were deceived by the serpent. They were told many lies, but the underlying lie they believed was that they did not need God, that they could also be God, in fact be their own God! They could make their own rules, and really be free! How delicious and delightful that sounded to their ears! They were tempted to doubt God's words and motive, and actually believed the serpent's words over God's words. They trusted the "new word." And far worse, they suspected God's motives, that He was controlling them, not loving them, that he was withholding and denying them knowledge and experience and limiting their freedom.

What is so terrifying to me is that we do the exact same thing! No matter what our temptations may be, and we all have different vulnerabilities to the lie, we ultimately have a choice to believe or not believe God's word to us. The Father sent Jesus, His only Son, into our exile here on planet earth, not to condemn the world but to save the world. After Jesus' death and resurrection, the Father fulfilled His promise to send the Holy Spirit to literally live within us. Why? So we can be constantly led by God's own Spirit to help us on our journey back home. We were created to love God and to surrender our lives to the Father, Son and Holy Spirit. That is not debatable, it is our reality. So, when we do not surrender to the one true God, we end up surrendering to any number of the many false gods that compete for our worship. You may even think you do not have any god, false or otherwise, but your god is whatever you turn to in your moment of need.

It might be helpful to look at some specific ways we can surrender to God, the Father, the Son and the Holy Spirit, that will surely set us free.

• *Surrender to the Father's love for us.* We can only do this once we dare to believe that God's motive is to love us, that His will leads us to the greater good, and that He has a plan - a good plan - for our lives. But we must surrender to His love for it to begin to heal us and take away our fear. "Not my will but Thy will be done," Jesus prayed in the other garden, the Garden of Gethsemane. What is Jesus saying by this? He is saying that, because I trust you Father, beyond my own understanding and feelings, I know you want to lead me to what will make me whole, and set me free. And set as many of your creation free as possible. That is Your Will.

• *Surrender to Jesus as Lord.* Jesus is our Savior, because of what He did for us by surrendering His life on the cross, giving us the great gift of Salvation. But He is not always our Lord – He only becomes our Lord when we make Him that in our lives – when we surrender our lives to Him. Who sits on the throne of your heart? I remember being on a retreat and using my imagination to try to "picture" my heart. I saw an image of my heart…it was a room with a huge throne in it, and on the throne was this little girl swinging her legs, twirling her hair thinking and saying "I want this…I want that…*ooh* look over there…wow! Look at that!" And I saw Jesus kneeling on the floor, looking up at the little girl (me). My heart broke…Jesus my Savior on the floor? Why was Jesus on the floor? In my imagination I saw myself slowly slip off the throne and lower myself down to the floor. I looked down, kind of ashamed, and I motioned for Jesus to sit on the throne, where He belonged. And you know what He did next? He scooped me up and put me on His lap! That imagery has stayed with me for years, because it showed me how I needed to allow Jesus to be not only my Savior, but my Lord. I am invited to make Jesus the Lord of *my* life! This seems to involve letting my heart break for love of Jesus.

• *Surrender to the Holy Spirit,* who dwells within us to guide us home, who comforts us in our afflictions, and afflicts us in our comfort when we get too comfortable with the "I want this" and the "I want thats" that the world deceptively and relentlessly keeps enticing us with. Jesus says that the Holy Spirit will be our Comforter, to bring the consolation of the love of God to us in the midst of our tribulations. The Spirit is our Counselor, gently revealing truth to us, the truth about ourselves and the deceptions swirling around us, and will remind us of everything Jesus taught us while He walked the earth. The Spirit dwells within us to whisper the loving word of God so we know we are not alone. And the Holy Spirit convicts us of our sin. Fr. David Pivonka, Franciscan Friar of the Third Order Regular, says that the Holy Spirit does not convict us of our sin to condemn us, but rather to convert us! The motive is love, not to take away our freedom, but to protect it! The Spirit whispers to us as we seek to make decisions and find our true purpose, and as we seek to help others and to serve our community with the gifts He has given us. We will always have a choice as to how we will respond to what we hear, but God keeps His promise to perpetually keep speaking His Word to us, right in our very own hearts.

Therefore, when we surrender to the God who made us, it is our false selves that die, not our true self. That is why it is not a contradiction that the way to true freedom is to surrender ourselves to our God, and then to allow Him to reveal to us who He made us to be, and let Him gently peel away the layers of the false selves that bury us, the false identities that the serpent keeps trying to create. That is the freedom we all long for.

PRAYER

The Lord taught me to bless myself in a new way. Before, when I would bless myself, I would make the sign of the cross so rapidly, mumbling "Father Son and Holy Spirit" so fast that it all blurred into one big nonsensical word. I didn't even realize what I was doing and saying, so I really kept missing the blessing. He taught me to make the sign of the cross slowly and deliberately, and say with each move of my hand:

"In the name of the Father, who loves and cares for me,

In the name of the Son, who died to set me free, and

In the name of the Holy Spirit, who comforts and empowers me."

Try blessing yourself this way, making the sign of the cross, and feel the love, freedom and power of God who wants to bless you in His name.

Amen.

And I Remember Your Sin No More

This entry is short and sweet...rather, short and bittersweet.

Do you know that feeling you get, after the fact, that you have made a grievous wrong turn? One that changes the direction of your life circumstances and sets you on a course that you cannot change? And you realize that all the remorse, and all the regret, cannot get that moment back when the wrong decision was made.

I had such a moment when we were selling our CT home. A buyer came along and we thought the offer was from the Lord's hand, an answered prayer. It came to us on Good Friday no less, as we pulled into our driveway after attending Good Friday services. The Lord had been faithful to us! The offer came a day after we put the house on the market. We even had a price in mind that we would accept, and the offer came in at exactly that price. Even as I write this, I cannot understand how I put aside all these "God fingerprints" to make a decision consistent with advice from our very knowledgeable, and very experienced realtor. Logic dictated that perhaps this could be risky, and we would take the house off the market only to have to list it again later when the market would be less than ideal. After that offer, we did not ever receive another one as good. We tried to contact the people that made the original offer and they were no longer interested...you can't get the moment back. We suffered for months, had to lower our asking price, and hire window washers, and cleaning ladies to make the house look even more appealing based on feedback from open houses that happened well after our first offer. My husband even closed off a closet in the master bedroom with sheetrock to provide a longer expanse of wall to be able to accommodate a king bed with 2 night tables! We eventually sold it, but I cannot deny we made a bad choice.

As I was talking to God about this one early morning before getting out of bed, telling Him how sorry I was that I did not accept the beautiful gift he had offered us, and even worse, that I failed to RECOGNIZE His hand and His ways of working in my life, I remembered the story of Esau. And it made me cry.

Esau is the older brother that sold his birthright to Jacob for a bowl of porridge. He was so hungry and wanted the porridge that he gave up his position in the family and all the rights and God given promises that went with that. Afterward he was heartsick, and could never get that moment back, nor his rightful position and blessings. What can heal such a wound?

There is truly a need to repent when we fail to choose God's way over our own selfish desires, or over someone else's way. I was able to find peace when I acknowledged that I did in fact sin. So many loved ones told me "maybe it was the right decision" but in my heart I knew it was not. There is NO COMFORT in being told you didn't do anything wrong when the Holy Spirit is convicting you of a wrong choice!

The only consolation comes when you acknowledge your mistake and allow yourself to hear God whisper the words "I forgive you." And even more, when He says "And I remember your sin no more".

Consequences remain, but the blessings of God in your life are freed up to flow again. May the Lord use my mistake as a gift for you.

PRAYER

Dear Lord, help us to learn to recognize your ways and the blessings from Your hand in our life.

I lift up to you the prayer request that is most gnawing in my spirit at this moment. Holy Spirit, shed light into my mind and show me where God is leading me. Help me to put aside my own logic, my own immediate needs for satisfaction, and the wisdom of the world to be able to listen to your whisper in my heart. Is there an answer You are speaking to me now, possibly even using my own words when I first talked to You about this?

Help me not to exchange Your blessing for a very short term bowl of porridge.

In the Name of Jesus,

Amen.

PART IV.

SOME "GOOD GOD" QUESTIONS

Am I Saved? Am I Safe?

There are lots of jokes about evangelicals asking the "Are you saved?" question, yet I believe it is a question that actually evokes fear at a deeper level. We jokingly say "sure", or "who knows", but the question touches a deep part of us, the part that has to admit that lurking in our subconscious is a fear of death, our death to be exact, and a fear of the unknown. Despite our faith, we still doubt that God really loves us, and we wonder if we are safe, not only here and now, but even more so, after our last breath here on earth.

Jesus died for us all, but not all accept His death as being a personal gift of salvation for their soul. It is easy to say that Jesus is my savior, but far more involved to say He is Lord of my life. To really accept the gift of salvation offered to us by God the Father through Jesus His Son, we have to die to our self. He surrendered His life on the cross for us, we too have to surrender our control of our own life to Him.

I think that is where Christians get caught up in terminology. Declaring Jesus is my Savior is one fundamental decision I make in a moment of time, whereas declaring Jesus is My Lord takes a lifetime of decisions.

A better question to ask rather than "Are you saved?" is "Is Jesus Lord of your life?" Jesus may very well be your Savior, but is He your

Lord? My belief is that until Jesus becomes our Lord, we will always question our salvation and wonder if we are truly safe with regard to eternal life.

That leads us to another question…what does it mean to say "Jesus is My Lord?" Simply put, it is the answer to the question "Do you love Jesus?" Have you come to the place where you realize how great is His love for you? When you realize how much He loves you - as you are, not as you should be - you begin to love Him in return. That loving Him in return is very much the essence of making Jesus your Lord.

Perhaps the real evangelical question we should be asking one another is "Do you love Jesus?"

PRAYER

Lord Jesus, thank you for dying for me. Even if I was the only person in the world You would have given your life for me, so that I could come home to the Father after my death. I admit I don't really grasp the depth of your love, but I accept it and ask that it permeate my inner being. That it touch those places of fear, guilt and shame within me.

Jesus, right now, in this moment, I declare that I LOVE YOU.

I love you Jesus. You are my Savior and I want to make you Lord of my life.

I want to learn how to turn over my will to yours. I want to learn to let go of things I hold onto that only serve to keep me separated from You and Your love for me.

In the words of good ol' Billy Graham Sinner's Prayer:

Dear Lord Jesus,

I know that I am a sinner, and I ask for Your forgiveness.

I believe You died for my sins and rose from the dead.

I turn from my sins and invite You to come into my heart and life.

I want to trust and follow You as my Lord and Savior.

If you have prayed this prayer from your free will and heart, know that you are safe in the arms of Christ Jesus, the Lord, here on earth and thereafter.

Amen.

Who is the Holy Spirit Anyway?

We are all at this moment "Now", coming from some moment prior to this, "Past", and continuing on to some moment after, "Future." We are coming from prior circumstances, often thinking of things we think we should be doing, or thinking about somewhere else we should or would rather be. It is a challenge to remain in the moment "now", to be "present to the present moment". What does this have to do with the Holy Spirit?

It is in the moment now that we directly encounter God in the person of the Holy Spirit. When we quiet our minds and pray, we are able to get in touch with the Holy Spirit that is within us. If we are honest, we might say that's all well and good, but…Who is the Holy Spirit? We have been taught, theologically, that the Holy Spirit is the third person of the blessed Trinity. Does that explain it for you? Probably not!

When we try to wrap our mind around a Trinity of three persons making up One God, it is beyond our natural abilities to comprehend such an identity. In John Chapter 1, we actually see the presence of all three persons in the Trinity when Jesus is baptized by John – we see Jesus being baptized, the dove hovering over Him, and the Father's voice from a cloud speaking "This is my beloved Son in whom I am well pleased." We can picture the person of God the Father, and we can picture the person of Jesus the Son, but how do you picture this third person? The Holy Spirit is often called the forgotten God because we really don't think much about the Spirit as a person.

There are several symbols used to represent the Spirit:

- Water – like a flowing river or a well that never runs dry;

- Fire – which inflames us and consumes us but does not destroy us, like Daniel in the furnace; Breath – the nearness of God (what is closer to you than your own breath?), and the source of Life;

- Dove – a symbol of peace and grace soaring through the skies of our world.

In the Old Testament, the Holy Spirit is mentioned in Genesis 1 when God created the world and the Spirit hovered over the darkness. The Spirit also hovers over people, such as the prophets, and anoints them for a specific service. In the New Testament, the Gospel of John says the most about the Holy Spirit, and the Holy Spirit is operating within and through the person of Jesus. Very different than the external hovering of the Spirit, the Spirit is now within a man. That was God's plan before the fall. He breathed into Adam, His first creation, imparting His own Spirit to Adam. The Holy Spirit was within Adam and Eve, until they sinned and thus became defiled; the holiness of God could no longer dwell within them. When Jesus died for us on the cross, His blood cleansed us from sin and made us able again to receive the Holy Spirit to dwell within us, as living tabernacles – a resting place - for God's presence.

Jesus promised that His Father would send us the Holy Spirit after His ascension back to heaven. In John 14: 15-31 He tells His disciples "...the Helper, the Holy Spirit, whom the Father will send in My name, He will teach you all things, and bring to your remembrance all that I said to you." This was a great comfort to the disciples when Jesus promised them that they would never again be alone or without the presence of the Holy Spirit, however unable they were to really understand how or when.

I like to reflect on the breath of God. On the cross, in John 19 we hear Jesus say "It is finished", then He *breathed* His last. Where did this Holy Breath of Jesus go? It was released from the cross in order to be received by those of us who believe and are baptized in His name.

We cannot follow God's plan without God's power. When we read the Acts of the Apostles - the forgotten gospel – we can see the difference the indwelling of the Holy Spirit makes.

In Acts 1, Jesus told the disciples to wait in Jerusalem until the power of the Holy Spirit came upon them. Like us, I'm sure they didn't understand what exactly they were waiting for. They probably wondered how they would know when it happened! Then during the Feast of Pentecost, when they were all gathered in the upper room, there was an undeniable experience of power exploding over them. There was a shaking, and a mighty wind that brought tongues of fire over each person.

After this, Peter is empowered to preach. Not only are his words inspired, but he has a newfound courage to speak these words. In the Book of Acts, we see that the disciples were given the power to heal the lame beggar. Peter says to him "Silver or gold I do not have, but what I do have I give to you. In the name of Jesus of Nazareth, rise up and walk!" (Acts 3:6).

Crowds gathered to be there when Peter walked by, because even Peter's shadow could heal! (Acts 5:15) The same power that was in Jesus was in Peter. And in you and me: the Holy Spirit. The Spirit desires to transform us from ordinary to extraordinary; helping us to become more like God...not becoming gods, but becoming God-like, in His image.

PRAYER:

What is my relationship with the Holy Spirit?

Reflection: Jesus said that the Holy Spirit would empower us with supernatural ability to live the Gospel. Some of the gifts of the Holy Spirit are:

• The power to know: wisdom, knowledge, and discernment

• The power to speak: speaking in tongues, prophecy, interpretation of tongues

• The power to act in the supernatural: supernatural faith, healing, performing miracles

What gifts do you most need from the Holy Spirit at this time in your life?

Reflection: Jesus said that the Holy Spirit would bring to our memory the words that Jesus taught - what is the Holy Spirit bringing to your memory? What might the Holy Spirit be teaching me, or trying to teach me?

Reflection: Jesus also reassured them that they didn't have to be anxious about how to remember all that He had taught them:

John 16: 5-22   "But when He, the Spirit of truth, comes, He will guide you into all the truth..."

When was I guided by truth...what did it feel like?

Amen.

3

Who Told You That You Were Naked?

In Genesis 3, we hear of the conversation between the serpent and Eve, and the horror of sin captured simply in two words: The Fall. The serpent asks Eve "did God really tell you not to eat of the fruit of any of the trees in the garden?" Eve replies that they can eat the fruit from all of the trees, with one exception: they cannot even touch, let alone eat, from the tree in the middle of the garden, or else they will die. This was the tree of the knowledge of good and evil.

That was pretty clear instruction from God – nothing ambiguous there! Eve, and her husband Adam, enjoyed a close relationship with God, taking daily walks together in the garden - God who is the Creator of all living things! It seems very unlikely that she would ever have had any reason to doubt God's word or instruction, or motive. Yet, the only thing the serpent had to say was "you will not die!" And Eve put her trust in the serpent, and believed the lie, rather than trusting God and His word to her. Why? It is almost absurd when you think about it. What was her vulnerability? Why did the lie appeal to her more than the truth? Why wasn't her relationship with God enough for her?

We also know that after she ate of the tree, she enticed Adam to do the same. Again we see in Adam the fickle loyalty of God's beloved to God's word; although he is less comfortable about it, he still chooses to follow Eve and eats the fruit as well. How could this be when their only experience of God was as Creator, the Giver of life and blessings; God as Beloved, the Giver of unconditional Love; and God as Friend, the Giver of companionship? But there was one other "biggy"… God was also the Giver of one commandment.

After eating the fruit (rather believing the serpent over God), they went into hiding. They tried to hide from God, who sees all and knows all, in God's garden! Sounds ridiculous but we do the same thing.

When Adam and Eve did not show up for their daily walk with God, He calls out to them "Where are you?" I'm sure God saw where they were hiding but apparently it was important to ask them the question…the first God question. They likely were not sure how to answer. They replied that they were hiding because they were naked! Now this is very interesting because they have always been naked! But now, somehow, they know that they are. God asks the next million dollar question…a question that will echo through all of time through all of humanity. "WHO TOLD YOU THAT YOU WERE NAKED?"

Was it bad to be naked?

Apparently when God created Adam and Eve, and gave them everything they needed, clothing wasn't part of the package. And they were blissfully ignorant of the fact that there was any other way. Can you imagine a world where we would not even know we were naked?

As we well know, Eve's act of disobedience, and her choice to trust the serpent – an "other," rather than God - unleashed a whole slew of ways that humanity would now be condemned to die. The serpent's declaration that they would not die "was the beginning of Fake news!"

There is the obvious consequence of physical death, and therefore our mortality, but there are also the other not so obvious "deaths" that are also upon God's creation that humanity would come to discover; e.g. sickness, pain, misunderstanding, conflict, suffering, depression, addiction, violence, famine, natural disasters, to name a few.

It seems that self-consciousness was also unleashed...the knowledge of good and evil...about their own selves! For the first time they saw themselves as other, as different even from each other, and began to hear that inner voice that is insecure and afraid – is it ok? Am I ok? They cover themselves with fig leaves to hide their most intimate selves. As do we. This self- consciousness – knowing we are naked – and God's question "who told you that you were naked" has morphed into other questions relevant to our times, such as:

- Who told you that you were fat?
- Who told you that you were ugly?
- Who told you that you are stupid?
- Who told you that you will never amount to anything?
- Who told you that you are a failure?
- Who told you that you are unlovable?
- Who told you that you do not belong?
- Who told you that God does not love you anymore?

The question "Who told you that you are naked?" is one of those God questions that causes us to freeze in silence when asked, because we realize that the answer eludes us, and we are forced to look inward, which is when we realize that we really don't know what has happened to us, or what will happen to us in the future. And we are painfully aware that we have sin within us. We are cognizant not only of our nakedness, but of the fact that there is still this part of us that wants to, and chooses to, walk away from God.

That is when we hear the voice of the Accuser, telling us that there is no way back, so we might as well go all the way away...

It takes us awhile to realize that, but in His great love for us, and rescue plan, God offers us the choice to turn around and come back home. God will always hope that once we see our nakedness, and our sinful nature, that we will choose to clothe ourselves with the blood of our Savior.

Rabbi Eric Tokajer wrote a brilliant essay that I recently read in Charisma News looking at morality in our world today, including (especially) in our Christian churches. He speaks about the false doctrine that has crept into the church that we no longer need to pay attention to the Old Testament, and in particular, we no longer need to follow the Ten Commandments; regardless of the fact that Jesus says in the gospels that He did not come to abolish the Law but rather to fulfill it. Rabbi Tokajer says this is the oldest lie in the book! Satan in the form of a serpent told that same lie to Eve – only at that point there was only *one* commandment - when he told her that she didn't have to follow God's commandment not to eat of the tree! Ecclesiastics 1: 9 states "There is nothing new under the sun...."

God's question to Adam and Eve shows us how important it is sometimes to wrestle with the right question rather than have all the answers. Like when Jesus asks the disciples "who do people say that I am?" And they chuckle and enjoy the wide variety of answers to that question – it was an easy question – they just reported what they heard. But then Jesus asks the God question..."but who do YOU say that I am?" This question silenced them in their tracks; they were forced to look within, not only for the answer to the presented question who do you say that I am, but it also goes deeper to the motivation behind the answer...*why* do I say what I say?

This reminds me of God's first question to Adam and Eve after the fall..."WHERE ARE YOU?" We know now that the one who told us we are naked and therefore no longer welcome to take a walk in the garden with our God, is the father of lies, the accuser, the one who roams about the world seeking to devour all those who love God and want to be in relationship with Him. The truth is that God asks us where we are so we can begin to find our longing for Him, and our desire to return to the place where we are indeed most welcome.

PRAYER

Enter into the presence of the Lord who made you, who has a plan for your life, and who covers your nakedness with His love. All shall be well if we turn towards His embrace that always waits for us; and if we turn away from all the voices that lead us away from Him. Many hands reach out for our attention…take the hand that is pierced for your transgressions and come home.

Conclude with this prayer of St. Julian of Norwich (bold and italics emphasis mine):

In you, Father all-mighty,

We have our preservation and our bliss.

In you, Christ, we have our restoring and our saving,

You are our mother, brother and Savior.

In you, our Lord the Holy Spirit,

Is marvelous and plenteous grace.

You are our clothing;

For love you wrap us and embrace us.

You are our maker, our love, our keeper.

Teach us to believe that by your grace all shall be well

And all shall be well,

And all manner of things shall be well.

Amen.

Amen.

4

Can I Enjoy Paradise if My Loved Ones Aren't There?

While enjoying a month in St. Croix, a tinge of homesickness for loved ones back in New England crept in, and I felt a kind of ache inside that was almost like a feeling of guilt, however irrational that would be. I felt so grateful to have this blessing, sitting on a balcony overlooking the ocean, my idea of paradise here on earth, and was keenly still aware of the challenging situations that I left behind (not to mention that my family and friends were in a real cold weather spell that January!) These feelings actually got in my way of enjoying the moment God had provided for me and my husband. Then the question floated into my mind – will I be able to enjoy heaven if my loved ones aren't there?

As our desire and ability to love actually comes from God, I trust that these feelings of love and responsibility to my loved ones is for this time on earth. I am called to love them and pray for them as long as I have breath and the ability to intercede. As much as I long for the Lord Jesus Christ to return in all His glory, I understand the Father's heart in this matter – He is waiting for every soul possible to want Him and turn away from sin and choose His pathway home, faith in Jesus the Christ. When I align my heart to the Father's loving heart in this regard, I don't want to leave anyone behind, and they are all worth waiting for.

How are we supposed to pray? How do you find the right words to say to change a heart? How do you say the right thing to save a person or a situation? I have often felt this and said to the Lord "I can't save [name of person] – I can't even save myself!" It is then that I am truly set free to pray in the power of the Holy Spirit, because I can trust my prayers in tongues. I get out of the way and invite the Holy Spirit to pray for my intentions through me. I cannot change anyone including myself. Sometime I will catch myself thinking "I can't do ANYTHING! All I can do is pray!" Yes!!!! That IS all I can do and you know what? That is everything! The power of my prayer IS doing something. I may not see it but in the spiritual realm, with my faith in Jesus, I am moving mountains for the sake of this person.

I trust that when the Father chooses to send His beloved Son Jesus to return to earth, not as a babe in the manger but as the undisputed, recognizable King and Lord of all, that I will be able to finally let go of the burdens of love that called for intercession for those that do not know or want to know Him. I will trust God that everyone that wants to be with Him in heaven is there. Those that do not want to be with God do not have to be.

I look at the ocean now and see the endless waves and sunrise and moonrise, and realize that His timing really is perfect, and I need to trust in His time, not my own. And trust that His love and yearning for my loved ones is far greater than my own. Until then I will continue to pray for blind eyes to open, deaf ears to hear, muted voices to speak, and all of creation to find the God that loves them so dearly.

PRAYER

Who is the Lord bringing to your mind at this moment?

What do you see or believe about this person? It is important to identify what the burden is that you are carrying for this person or their situation.

Submit your perception to the Lord and ask Him to show you what He sees about this person or situation.

Ask the Holy Spirit to guide your prayer...to give you the words to pray...for this person.

Amen.

5

Who Do You Say that I Am?

For me, there can be no more haunting question from Jesus in the sense of probing the depths of my beliefs and my soul, and revealing fears, doubts, failures and my testimony to Jesus as my Lord and Savior.

Jesus asks this question of His disciples in Gospels (Matthew 16:15. Luke 9:20), and it was Simon (Peter) who answered "You are the Christ, the Son of the Living God." It seems to me that Jesus was profoundly touched by Peter's response, and He immediately affirms Simon (Peter) by affirming the truth of his declaration, telling him that his insight and proclamation were beyond human capability, and that this truth could only have been revealed to him by the Father alone. Jesus then renames Simon "Peter", meaning "the Rock", and goes on to say that He will build His church upon this rock. I am not sure if Jesus meant He would build His church upon Peter himself, or upon the truth that Peter proclaimed. Either way it was a probing moment for the disciples that left eleven of the twelve speechless.

Each of us who follow Jesus is called to answer that very same question. Who do I say that Jesus is by my words, my actions and my life's proclamation? I think we will wrestle with that question until the day we die. What we choose to speak or emphasize might even change throughout our lives as we experience our personal relationship with Jesus change concurrent with living out our life's circumstances. There are the basic tenants of our faith that we can probably all recite in answer to this question, based on the Creed we profess: Jesus was born of a virgin, died on a cross, and rose from the dead, then ascended to His Father in heaven. But the question goes deeper than that...the question is more about the strength of my belief and my "faithfulness to my faith," as it were.

Each year as I hear and contemplate the reading of the Passion on Palm Sunday, something new seems to strike me from the Gospel account. Partly because the liturgical church reads a different account of the Synoptic Gospels each year for 3 years, and reads the Gospel of John on Good Friday. Each author tends to stress different aspects of the Passion, likely what was witnessed and what was experienced in the author's own heart. But even if the same account was read each year, I think that the Holy Spirit causes us to hear what we need to hear on a given year, or at a given moment, related to our circumstances and our relationship with God. This year I was struck by the different testimonies given to the Sanhedrin in Mark's gospel by witnesses who supposedly saw and heard Jesus speak. Mark summarizes this account by saying:

"But their testimonies did not agree"

This made me reflect on my own testimony about who I say that Jesus is...and how contradictory it can be based on my state of mind or emotions on a given day. But even beyond my potentially inconsistent nature, this scripture also made me think about our Christian church today (in 2018 as I am writing this entry). The testimonies of the various Christian churches no longer agree! How scary and sad that is. Starting with the obvious, the Christian church has so many different denominations (each one created to defend a certain interpretation of God's Word) and lacks love and respect for each other, that the witness (aka testimony) to the watching secular world is ludicrous. Some ordain women, some cannot. Beliefs about the Eucharist vary from bread alone to the actual presence of the living Christ, and depending on what the church believes, there are rules that go along with that. My husband said something that I thought was profound when we were attending an ecumenical service one day between Lutherans and Catholics, which are not very far apart denominationally, but the differences have grown more and more with each new generation. My husband said "until we can learn how to eat together (aka share Eucharist), we cannot unite." Something as simple as sharing a meal together is wrought with division.

Even more frightening to me is that you can find a Christian church that not only proclaims that homosexuality is not wrong, but even ordains ministers, priests and bishops that are actively living in gay relationships, while other Christian churches state that God loves the homosexual, but hates the sin of homosexuality, and that we are to love the sinner but hate the sin. This is no small difference of opinion and calls the Word of God into question. This confusion in the church's positions is wreaking havoc, especially for our younger generation who look for guidance when they are struggling with their identity, sexuality, and calling in this world. They seek healing and wisdom from elders but discover that one church says it is fine, do as you feel, while another church says it is wrong and you are evil, while another says "God can heal even this." I am of that belief, that God can heal all of our sin when we have the courage and humility to name our sin and bring it to Him to be healed. But if the testimonies of our Christian churches do not agree, then which churches are preaching Jesus Christ, the Word made flesh? Which church is bearing false witness?

When we consider that in the Gospel of John, chapter 17, Jesus's last prayer was that we His followers would be one as Jesus is one with the Father, it is very disturbing that this could have happened within the Body of Christ. It is as if Jesus knew that we would become divided, and that our testimony to the world in answer to the questions of the human heart, even the question "what did Jesus Christ say and do" would become contaminated with wrong teaching. Thank God Jesus also said to Peter the Rock, that "the gates of hell will not prevail against it" [His Church]. (Matthew 16:18)

May we never stop praying for unity in the Body of Christ. Can you imagine if all the Christian churches were united in their testimony as to "Who Do You Say that I Am?" Truly the gates of hell would be consumed by our light.

PRAYER

Let us pray with the Prayer of St. Francis for this reflection:

"Lord, make me an instrument of your peace.

Where there is hatred, let me sow love.

Where there is despair, hope.

Where there is injury, pardon.

Where there is doubt, true faith in you.

O Master grant that I may never seek

So much to be consoled as to console.

To be understood as to understand,

To be loved as to love with all my soul.

For it is in giving that we receive,

In forgiving that we are pardoned, and

In dying we are born to eternal life."

Lord Jesus, I offer you my Self…the person you ask "Who do you say that I am?" Please heal the broken, fragmented and conflicting beliefs within my own heart, and in the Heart of Your Church.

Amen.

6

What If?

Since retiring, I am surprised to find that more and more of my friends have become atheists, most of them former Catholics. They are very good people, better than many professing Christians I know, better than me! This reality has baffled me, and even paralyzed me, and silenced me from sharing my faith. It has caused me to question, not so much my faith, because thanks be to God, that seems to be a gift I've been given and it remains rock solid. But I am feeling a deep loneliness because it is harder and harder to share my deepest self with my closest friends. It is stressful to pretend, and I am not very good at small talk. It is painful to long to share the beautiful Jesus that I know personally, especially knowing how much He loves them, too. It is hard to find words to help people separate the bad church experiences they may have had, which are very real and damaging, from the loving God who seeks a relationship with them. I too am frustrated with the Christian churches; all of them. They are so unable to welcome even one another from other denominations, or different political parties (that is fodder for another book), that the hypocrisy of the love they preach about rings out much louder than saying the "God words" correctly.

My atheist friends believe in goodness, and in being good. I ask them "how do you define "good"? How do they know if they are doing or being good? What standard do they use? I don't get a crisp answer to that, except that there is an innate sense of right and wrong. What if that sense can only come from God, and the image of God that each one of us was created in? I also heard someone say at recent dinner conversation that we were all born innocent. If that were true, where does the will come from that chooses that which is "not good" in the atheists "belief" system? For Christians, we believe that we were intended to be created absolutely beautiful and innocent, but that because of the reality of sin, we are all infected as it were with the original sin of our first parents. It is in our spiritual DNA. We can't get rid of it on our own. It may seem a preposterous story to believe, but we cannot deny that we see evil at work even in our own heart, not only in the world out there, and we cannot deny that there is sickness and death. We cannot deny that everyone must and indeed does die. That was never God's original plan for His creation.

None of this answers the question "how can people who don't believe in God be so good?" That got me to wondering…perhaps the evil one does not tempt them in the same way that believers are tempted. They are tempted and encouraged to remain in their unbelief. Satan has a lot of goods to offer while we are exiled here on planet earth. And he offers them abundantly, except with a barb of death that is hidden to the eye.

Which led me to a series of "What if?" questions…

What if instead of being tempted to "do bad," unbelievers are tempted not to believe in the God who created them, loves them and died to save them from evil? Each of us is infected differently with this bad DNA upon our entry into our temporary exile here on planet earth. We all have a unique vulnerability and soft spot to the serpent's offers.

What if God loved us so much that He really did come to us on planet earth in human form, to take on that bad DNA for the purpose of finally destroying it?

What if He knew that the only way to break the power of the vicious cycle of sin and death over His children was to take it on Himself, including death?

What if the beaten and bloody Body of Christ, before He even was nailed to the cross, is a visual image of the effect that sin (aka the bad DNA) has on us? We don't see ourselves as ever looking that way, but what if that is how we look in the spiritual realm when our sin is not repented of and brought to the cross?

And what if in so doing, Jesus became the only antibody against this bad DNA? What if we had to get injected with the "Jesus antibody" to be able to fight back and survive? So that like Him, when we eventually have to die, it will be a passing on to the next life, the one that was originally intended for us?

What if the Good News is true? That the God who made us loves us so much that He found a way to save us from the spread of this horrible DNA of sin. He sent Jesus the Christ to be the antidote to sin. Jesus was crucified, died, was buried, and rose from the dead, thereby conquering the finality of death for those who believe in Him.

What if hell is a real place where there is no God...no sense of sanity, reason, kindness or a plumb line for right and wrong?

What if I am wrong and there really is no God, or right and wrong? That "what if" question I can answer. I will have spent my life knowing the joy and peace of having Jesus as my constant companion, never leaving me or forsaking me through all of life's trials and tribulations. I will have experienced healing from wounds inflicted upon me by other people's sin, or my own. I will have known a deep love and peace beyond my understanding. I would have seen small and big miracles, and answered prayers that I cannot deny were real interventions into my life after I prayed for help. I will have spent my life trying to grow into a more loving person, even trying to love and forgive my enemies. I will have lived unafraid of death, knowing I will eventually find myself in my Father's kingdom, with a seat at His banquet table. You know what? I can live with that!

But, to my unbelieving friends, family and humanity…What if you are wrong?

PRAYER

Lord Jesus, thank you for the gift of faith. Those that have faith sense that they have a responsibility to pray and intercede for others who are still unaware. As Father Richard Rohr once said in a homily… "evangelization is like one beggar telling the other beggar where to find food." We are all hungry for God.

During the beautiful Good Friday liturgy, the entire Church prays a series of intercessory prayers, among which are prayers for those who do not believe in Christ, and for those who do not believe in God. Let us pray for them now:

Lord, I lift up to you now all those that I know that do not believe in God, or in you, Jesus. I stand in the gap of their unbelief and intercede for their eyes to be opened to the reality of you. Give them the grace to forgive old wounds and those who inflicted wounds from their experience of Church as children. Give them the grace to separate believing in You from their experience of church. Or from lack of any experience of church at all.

I pray that all will be restless to dare to believe, and to ultimately find, their personal relationship with the Living God.

This is not about your religion, or lack thereof. This is about your relationship with the Living God.

I pray

In the Name of Father, who loves and cares for me.

In the Name of the Son, Jesus Christ, who died to set me free. And

In the Name of the Holy Spirit, who comforts and empowers me.

Amen.

7

Why Should I Pray if God's Will Happens Anyway?

This is probably where the rubber meets the road in our walk with the Lord. This question taps into many other questions we have about God, and our relationship with Him. Another way to ask this question is "doesn't God control everything no matter what I do?" The short version of this question is "Why bother to pray?" For me, the short answer is if Jesus prayed, then so should we.

Sometimes it helps to look at extreme ends of a spectrum to find that sweet spot where Truth resides. One end of the prayer life spectrum is to approach prayer like a Christmas list to Santa; the other end of the spectrum is to not believe in God at all, and certainly not to ask for His intervention or favor or assistance. Let us look at how Jesus prayed.

Scripture says that Jesus rose early before dawn and went off to a quiet place to pray; namely, Jesus created time and a place that would allow Him to get as close to His beloved Father as possible. He would yearn to be with His Father, and sought His Father's will before setting off to begin His day. I imagine He asked "Father, what is on Your heart today?" This does not mean that we aren't supposed to ask God for what we need. Jesus teaches us in the Our Father prayer "Give us this day our daily bread, and forgive us our trespasses...and lead us not into temptation...deliver us from evil." Jesus also tells us that Our Father knows what we need before we even ask Him. But to reorient our thinking into belief that God indeed has a purpose for our day, and for our lives, is a new way to contemplate prayer.

Similar to the way Jesus stands at the door and knocks, waiting for us to invite Him in; I believe that when we pray, we open the door for God's will to be done here on earth as it is in heaven. Jesus taught us to pray this way "Thy kingdom come, Thy will be done", and in the Garden of Gethsemane He prayed "not my will but your will be done." This implies that Jesus had the choice to lay down His life, and we see clearly that He really preferred not to have to lay down His life. Somehow Jesus's prayer was necessary for Him to be able to go to the cross to die for our salvation.

What if our prayer life is supposed to be about offering the gift of ourselves as a vessel to allow God's kingdom to come here on earth as it is in heaven? We will probably never be able to grasp or comprehend the purpose and power of our prayers. Yet Jesus teaches us to pray this way, which tells us that our prayers and our seeking do matter to God, and to the building of His kingdom here on earth.

We all know first-hand what it is like not to feel like our prayers were answered the way we hoped they would be answered. We also likely have learned along the way that sometimes when our prayers are answered the way we wanted, and we made choices to help God "move that answer along", that was not necessarily a good thing! It has been a great freedom for me in my later years to not try to figure out the perfect prayer, or what to ask for. I have learned that the perfect prayer really is "Thy will be done". So I pray for the Father's will to be done, and that my actions and choices be guided in a way to meet the desires of my Father's heart. This is perfect prayer because if we trust in God, that His motives are pure love, and that He is constantly about bringing the lost into the kingdom of God, then I pray to be a channel of actions and words that can open the doors of the day to create the atmosphere for God's will to manifest in specific situations, even if I do not know how God intends to move or heal.

So whether or not sick people are healed or not healed, I can choose to pray for and trust in His will. When things seem to go from bad to worse when I pray, I can trust that there is a greater good at work; and the greatest good is that course of action that results in the most souls finding the love of God the Father, and salvation through Jesus Christ. All things work together for good towards this end.

So for me it again comes down to this. I either believe in the God that Jesus revealed, or I do not. If I do not, then I will live by luck, try to be a good person...or not, and die when my time is up, and hope for the best, or nothing at all. But if everything Jesus revealed is true, then my faith and trust in the Living God really did matter, a lot in fact, and my life will have had a purpose that I will only realize later when I am face to face with Him. I will see my life in the light of His kingdom; and I will be sitting at the Father's banquet table, eating the finest bread, drinking the finest wine, and relishing the finest of foods, in the eternal presence of our Father.

PRAYER

I can't think of a better prayer for the last prayer of this book than the Our Father prayer. It is the bow that I would like to wrap this book with.

Let us reflect on the words that Jesus chose to give His disciples when they asked Him to teach them how to pray:

Our Father...God isn't just God, He identifies Himself as my Father, my Dad, my Daddy, my Abba. No matter what my earthly father was to me, I have a Father who is perfect and who loves me perfectly.

*Who art in heaven…*God's kingdom is beyond planet earth, where I live. Therefore, His ways, His thoughts, His plan, His reasons, His perspective are way beyond anything I can ask or imagine.

*Hallowed be thy name.…*there is sacredness and power in the name of God. We are called to revere and praise His name. Praise helps us to remember that He is God, limitless and perfect, all knowing and all loving; for whatever is wrong or for whatever I or my loved ones need, for whatever my problem or circumstance may be…God is greater.

Thy Kingdom Come Thy Will be done, on earth as it is in heaven. This prayer shows our surrender to the fact that we cannot see everything, we cannot know everything, we cannot solve everything (or anything for that matter!), but that God's kingdom brings us what we long for…the ultimate Truth, eternal life, and the perfect Way to live that brings peace and unity and freedom from sickness for all.

Give us this day our daily bread. We do not need to ask for more than the present day's need. This allows us to grow in faith and trust that God will indeed provide every day. I do not recall who the original author of this quote was, but it is key to this part of the Our Father prayer. "If God fails me today, then it will be the first time." Let us grow in our faith that this is true and always will be.

Forgive us our trespasses as we forgive those who trespass against us. This is pretty self-explanatory, but it is good to remember that forgiving does not excuse wrong behavior, it just releases me from it so I don't keep living it over and over and over again. And once we repent of our sins, God also does not keep holding it over and over and over again. Forgiveness is Freedom to move on.

Lead us not into temptation. We pray not to be tempted because as Jesus said in Matthew's gospel, Mathew 26:41, "the spirit is willing but the flesh is weak." None of us wants to be tested in our sometimes frail commitment to the God we love.

Deliver us from evil. This prayer encompasses much: particularly it affirms our knowledge that there is a spiritual war; that there is an evil power, there is an adversary, Satan, who we are told in 1 Peter 5:8 "prowls around like a roaring lion, seeking someone to devour"; but that God is greater, even if we are not, in and of ourselves. We need God's protection from the fiery darts of the evil one as we live out our lives here on earth, and this part of the prayer acknowledges the supremacy of God over all powers that be.

For thine is the kingdom, the power and the glory, forever and ever.

Amen.

Acknowledgments

I thank my husband, Robert E. Jaquith, who was the editor of this book. He took my "Scraps" and provided the focus and structure that was needed, as he does time and time again in my life. His editorial comments, support and gentle promptings are what got this book to the finish line.

I also thank my niece Lynn Opare-Addo for her insightful comments on earlier entries in the book, and for her persistent encouragement to write my book.

And last but not least, I thank my publisher, Dove Christian Publishers/Inscript Books, for guiding me through the publishing process, and for their Statement of Faith which is what drew me to choose them as my publisher.

May the work of this team bear good fruit and be a blessing!

About the Author

Susan Ceraldi Jaquith has served in lay ministry since 1977, seeking to combine her faith journey with practical insights on how to live out our spirituality in the real world. She has served as a prayer group leader, facilitator of retreat days and workshops, and provided spiritual direction and pastoral counseling to those seeking to grow in their personal relationship with God. She worked as a part time counselor at Associated Counseling Professionals (ACP) in Hartford, CT from 1985 – 1995. She also served on the leadership team of the Catholic Charismatic Renewal for the Archdiocese of Hartford for over 20 years.

Concurrently, Sue enjoyed a successful 35 year engineering career as an engineer and manager, and retired from Westinghouse Electric Co. (formerly ABB and Combustion Engineering) in 2013. Sue is happily married to her husband Bob since 1992 and resides in Charlestown, RI.

CPSIA information can be obtained
at www.ICGtesting.com
Printed in the USA
JSHW030518080922
30034JS00004B/105